Frog Hollow Journal

Reality and illusion: the education of a Canadian family in the Shenandoah Valley, with some thoughts on the Beatitudes

by
James G. T. Fairfield

With illustrations by Norma Fairfield

iUniverse, Inc.
New York   Bloomington

iUniverse books may be ordered through booksellers or by contacting:

iUniverse
1663 Liberty Drive
Bloomington, IN 47403
www.iuniverse.com
1-800-Authors (1-800-288-4677)

Because of the dynamic nature of the Internet, any Web addresses or links
contained in this book may have changed since publication and may no longer be
valid. The views expressed in this work are solely those of the author and do not
necessarily reflect the views of the publisher, and the publisher hereby disclaims
any responsibility for them.

ISBN: 978-1-4401-2918-6 (sc)
ISBN: 978-1-4401-2920-9 (dj)
ISBN: 978-1-4401-2919-3 (ebook)

Printed in the United States of America

iUniverse rev. date: 3/25/2009

SCHOOL

Preface

From Red to Shenandoah

Kids in elementary school are impressionable; at least I seemed to be. January is an impressionable experience in rural Manitoba, arguably the coldest province in Canada. One or two other provinces might boast their below-zero records, but none have cared to match the consistent bitterness of Manitoba winters.

The windows of our one-room school were framed in sculptured ice; the condensed breath of thirteen steaming kids froze from the bottom up on the window panes. Even though the janitor sealed visible cracks with strips of heavy woolen felt, winds from the Arctic with nothing to stop them but a few thin poplar groves whipped around our little school building and shook its seams loose. The poplar-wood and coal furnace in the corner of the basement fought back, but ineptly, never pulling a better grade than C minus.

In that draft-ridden one-room school on the banks of the Red River, Mrs. Fredrickson taught me to love geography. She used a big map of the world on a roll she pulled down over the blackboard, a huge window-blind sort of thing painted in vivid reds and greens with indigo oceans and inland seas of lighter hue. She told stories of the Boer War and the charge of the Light Brigade at Crimea. In 1934, even under two feet of snow, we were still part of the British Empire, and Britannia ruled a good chunk of terrestrial real estate back then.

A sturdy Icelandic blonde, Mrs. Fredrickson came to Manitoba as a child. Like many first generation Canadians, she became a fierce loyalist and in her classroom gave preference to imperial history, but come January, she couldn't help herself. She fled to warmer subjects, and we studied the culture of the south. We drew maps of the major islands in the Caribbean and colored them with crayons. She read us a story about Stonewall Jackson in the Shenandoah Valley and tried to teach us to sing about the Shenandoah in harmony, anywhere from two or so parts on up—there were the thirteen of us.

We'd push back the desks in front of the blackboard near the vent from the furnace, and Mrs. Fredrickson would find the pitch with a tuning fork she kept in her desk. Every day through January we'd work up to "O Shenandoah, I long to see you...," and staring out the frost-rimed windows at the whitened landscape, my heart would fill with an unaccustomed, indescribable longing. I felt sad and elated and puzzled all at once —and I didn't know why. Not then. It was years before I knew what was missing.

※　※　※

One of the realities most of us wrestle with is the longing for Place—however we may think of it. Somewhere else, in some way, we will be truly "at home." A better climate. More satisfying job. Kinder friends. Happier circumstances.

We want this to happen to us but aren't able to map out how to get there from here. Come up rich for starters, maybe win the lottery. Then we can fire the boss, dump our problems, move to a better location, find more caring friends. So God, please let me hit the Big One.

But what if it doesn't happen the way I want it to, and I have to live with what I've got? "Sufficient unto the day is the evil thereof," or something like that. Success then becomes surviving what we learn about ourselves and the illusions we call existence. Yet it's hard to dismiss the illusions, if we're convinced they're the truth.

How do we cope with the human condition—illusions and all? The New Testament gospel of Matthew tells of a crowd gathered on a hillside, hoping to catch a miracle or two from Jesus. Calling the first part of what he said there the Beatitudes gives it a label, yet labels sometimes obscure the substance. Here were people trying to survive all manner of personal concerns: a mean boss, rebellious teenagers, a cheating spouse, too many taxes, a crippling disease. Some really needed a miracle and pushed close to Jesus. Others in the crowd were disciples, a short-hand term to describe individuals with a fierce determination to follow this man who seemed to have "something." Whatever it was he had, they wanted.

Jesus had a profound effect on people. He seemed to draw their longings for Place and for something better into a commitment to follow him until they found his reality and discovered the kind of kingdom he said was so near. But after 2000 years or so, what value does the understanding of some man called Jesus have for someone struggling with reality today?

Norma and I did not see our wants being met by Jesus, or any other religious figure for that matter. Religion fell into the category of a sidebar to an already overcrowded life, a spiritual hobby we couldn't afford. We were too preoccupied with babies and job demands and a tight budget to give religious explorations any room in our lives. We simply accepted the social climate of Canadian ideas and values—wherever they might have come from—as an adequate background to lean on and claim if anyone asked. We had yet to understand the full dimensions of reality and our place in it.

*　*　*

Since it's a personal thing, a journal can be pretty well anything it wants to be; this one tries to understand an evolutionary leap of the spirit, a metamorphosis in the essence of our being. Some people get into it without a lot of fuss. Others, like me, drag their heels all the way. It's never easy to change directions and face new responsibilities with untried motives after you've been living half a lifetime. So how does anyone recognize the landscape of a radical transformation in who we are and its new demands on our thoughts and actions? Especially when we can't anticipate what the transformation will look like?

I've grown leery of the term "religious conversion" since it carries so much old psychological freight. What we were to discover in Frog Hollow was a new way of thinking about "religion" and the evolutionary possibilities in the gospel of Jesus.

*　*　*

In order to preserve the well-earned privacy of our neighbors, I have changed some names and altered some circumstances; these days you never know who'll turn up full of curiosity and foolish questions when you're in the middle of canning tomatoes or fixing fence.

Having read such a declaration, you may question if these accounts can be believed. In certain circumstances most of us find factuality gets in the way of truth. For instance, anyone who has grappled with Biblical truth knows that it carries much more meaning than the words can hold. It's like beef jerky; the more you chew it, the bigger it gets.

Facts such as names, events, times, locations and explanations contain a sort of reality we call truth, but our neighbors are much more than these data and their illusions. So the lives herein you can count on; it's the facts you'll have to take with a grain of salt.

I'm not a historian. I didn't tape the stories on a recorder, take notes or ask for written accounts. If you're at Ray Hollar's shop where he's welding your broken brush cutter and a neighbor tells you he busted an axle on his tractor in a groundhog hole and starts a story on how his dog frustrated a groundhog, you don't say, "Wait 'til I get a pencil and paper."

That's the problem with oral history; it gets filtered through somebody's memory, sometimes a couple of other memories, including my own. And since there are days I'm lucky I remember my name, I can only apologize for telling the stories the way I recall them. Even the writers of the Bible had to deal with the problem, or so I'm told.

* * *

Norma and I were in our thirties when we moved to Virginia, and fairly new to the idea of trusting God to make sense out of life, with all the struggles for understanding that involves. We had four young children, an old car, little money and a lot to learn, especially about faith and its consequences.

Frog Hollow and its residents slowly exposed us to the meaning of life in the "kingdom of God," an ancient idea as much abused by its allies as by its adversaries. Christianity's friends sometimes live as if they believe Jesus didn't mean but half of what he said. I know I found much more than I could handle in what he taught, even in such condensed thoughts as the Beatitudes. So coming to grips with the reality—the "kingdom" he talked about—stayed well out on the periphery of my life. Even in church on Sunday. Or maybe especially in church on Sunday, when the divide between what I was doing with the rest of my life and what I believed of God and his realm seemed like an unbridgeable chasm.

We didn't know it at the time, but our move to Frog Hollow was to become a bridge for us, a providential gift with God's smile behind it. Frog Hollow and its residents eased us across the gap. It became not only a place where we lived but an explanation of who we were and what we might become by the grace of God.

*　*　*

Wherever we go, we drag a culture with us, family history as well as local customs and dialect. Norma and I came from Scots/Irish background, born and raised in Manitoba, Canada. While our children were in their early years at school, we began the moves which landed us in the Shenandoah Valley, home to a lot of people from somewhere else, also speaking the English language. But there any cultural similarity ended and our southern exposure began.

It's a long way from the Red River to the Shenandoah. A long, long way; fourteen hundred miles and several cultural shifts. Put a country boy from each region in a strange barn at night and together they could figure out where the door is, but not much else. I grew up on the Red River near its delta at the southern end of Lake Winnipeg where all the kids spoke "bungey," a heavily accented dialect with Scottish and Cree Indian roots. It flattened out a little when my parents moved us to the city of Winnipeg, and by the time Norma and I got married there, she could almost understand me.

John Schaefer grew up on a farm about a half-mile south of Frog Hollow, back in the hills along the Shenandoah Valley. When we moved into our first home in the Valley, John stopped by to invite our kids to a church youth cook-out and we understood about five words in ten. Yet we got the impression of a smiling, gentle, well-muscled youth with clear blue eyes, fair hair and a quick wit. But that's getting ahead of the journal's tales and the education in our reality.

* * *

Frog Hollow is an actual place in the foothills of western Virginia, where the Shenandoah gets one of its many starts in spring fed streams and wet weather runs. But it's not a name you'll find on a tourist map.

As we learned in the one room school in rural Manitoba, everybody everywhere knows the Shenandoah River. But here in Virginia, few even nearby know of Joe's Creek. On the one hand, it could be said that Joe's Creek *is* the Shenandoah, since somewhere down the creek's innumerable twists it becomes what it flows into. On the other hand, there are several hundred other creeks with similar or even better claims. Joe's Creek has only this singularity; it flows through Frog Hollow.

Not to be taken as a microcosm, Frog Hollow is what it is, uniquely so because of the people who live here. Furthermore, since the hollow's residents include more than people, the welfare of all must be considered: mockingbirds and cardinals, poultry and cattle, trees and wildflowers, deer and foxes and groundhogs. And dogs. As we found out, dogs are important residents in the hollow. Dogs like Shep.

In fact, I have to start with Shep, because he became so much a part of our lives. A dog is to new residents of the hollow as a cookbook is to a budding chef. Without a recipe a beginning cook might cobble a meal together, and without Shep we might have found our way around the hollow. But a good guide dog sure helped us get our bearings.

SHEPPY

1

Forecast: Change

No one can warn us of an impending thunderstorm quite like Shep. Our local television channel has its own meteorologist, and a couple of radio stations hire a meteorological service for accurate forecasts. In addition, we can dial two different telephone numbers for weather updates, but when it comes to an immediate storm warning, Shep takes the gold.

Sheppy can spot a thundershower a half hour away. Norma will be hanging some curtains on the line to freshen, then she'll take them down and put them back in the basket, because Sheppy is there, wrapped around her ankles. Most dogs are afraid of a storm, but Shep is paranoid about it, a craven coward.

We are not his first family. When he was six months old or thereabouts, Shep adopted us. One March morning of our first winter in Virginia, I looked out the kitchen door and saw a shadow under the pickup. I chased it away. After breakfast the shadow was back, so I roared at it again.

Next morning he was there once more. "Go on, get away! Get! Get!"

When I came back to the breakfast table, I wondered at the cool silence. It was early. People don't talk much at that hour of the morning. And likely it had nothing to do with the dog anyway. We didn't need a dog. We had just bought some sheep, and dogs run sheep. "He'd help guard our sheep, Daddy."

But we had a cat, too. Cats and dogs are like oil and water. "Mrs. Cat doesn't mind him, Daddy."

Was I being sandbagged? I didn't know it then, but our oldest son, Jim, had slipped some of his breakfast to the shadow under the truck. After the school bus left, Norma said maybe we should let him stay.

"But you don't like dogs!"

"I like this one," she said. "He's cute. And he's probably hungry. Let's keep him."

You can't argue with logic like that. I picked up a license and a collar, and when the children came home from school that evening, he was there to meet them. And from then on, he was there to love them when teachers were unfair and other kids were mean and even Mom and Dad didn't seem to understand.

We think somebody passing through dumped him off along the road to avoid paying the dog tax. We also figure he had tried to find a home at another place and they took a shot at him, because when Jim brought out his air rifle to shoot pigeons in the barn, Shep nearly had a breakdown. He put his tail down, then cried and wet and groveled and ran in circles all at once.

While he's still apprehensive about guns these days, it's not to the same degree. Now it's a roll of thunder that triggers old fears and he tries to sit in your lap.

But we can never get a long range forecast out of him.

* * *

It's difficult to forecast life, especially when you are becoming something new in your soul or spirit or psyche. When we began to sense the presence of God—whoever he or she was—it started with angst: *Life is good, so why do I feel so lousy?*

In the early 1950s we moved to Blair, a little Canadian village about a mile from the textile mill my father and four of my older brothers had bought in Preston, Ontario, about 50 miles west of Toronto. The original Fairfield & Sons mill and offices were in Winnipeg, and for the first three years I was expected to run the Ontario plant, heady stuff for a becoming-man in his twenties. Then two of the brothers moved east, and I slid back down to the bottom of the family totem pole (the younger of the two was 22 years my senior—I was a surprise my parents survived with the help of my older sister Anne, aged 20 when I was born).

When my brothers took over, I was given a job in sales which called for a fair amount of travel away from my family, covering the needle trades in Montreal and Toronto. I wasn't all that good at schmoozing with clients who knew so much more about woolen cloth than I did, but somebody had to carry around the samples and try to sell a mill run.

I really didn't like being away from Norma and our four young children. A comedy of major errors saw our company wind up in the temporary control of some accountants and lawyers in Toronto. I was offered a contract as sales manager of the business, with the understanding that I would spend at least six months of the year on the road.

From the distance of years, I know now that God was giving me an opportunity to choose a new life. Some men and women would have chosen the sales job and found their lives filled with grace. But something else was stirring in our lives, and I wound up deciding to finish my undergraduate degree, which had been interrupted by service in World War II, in Virginia instead.

*   *   *

We left Canada after the children's school year ended, and rented a small farm at the beginning of summer. Our first year in Virginia was a hectic time of adjustment for all of us. Then we bought the place we had been renting, and our hectic adjustments took a different shape. The children were willing to pitch in, doing massive amounts of work cleaning up and mending fences. The old barn had a nearly four-foot deep layer of hardened manure to dig out and spread around for fertilizer.

We'd seen the thistles growing in the fields that first summer—the place had been overgrazed and under cared for. The farm family next door warned us the pastures produced more thistles than forage, and suggested if we were going to be good neighbors, we'd dig them out or cut them down before they blossomed. And spread to their fields.

So that first spring, our second son, John, dug emerging thistles with a mattock every afternoon after school; yet the prolific weeds soon outgrew the boy. When school let out that summer there was a forest of prickly growth covering one section of the north pasture, thistle growth only a scythe or a brush-hook could handle. The sheep we'd bought simply tunneled through the canes, looking for something edible and not finding much. No grasses could grow where the barbed stalks stood almost seven feet high, shutting out light and absorbing the nutrients from the soil.

In spite of his willing nature, John felt overwhelmed by the size of the task he faced. I told him not to fuss; wasn't cutting them with a scythe as easy as digging them with a mattock? He looked at me, then out the window at the growth higher than his head.

"But Dad, those things are like trees! And the barbs go right through my shirt!" It was the first time he had complained.

Like the other children, John worked hard. That week

he had begun to build a wooden fence across the end of the garden and along a small pasture leading to the barnyard, a project he had planned by himself and seemed eager to complete. Norma reminded me quietly that he was working on a fence we sorely needed. He had other chores to do besides cutting thistles, and didn't I think he'd done enough?

I replied that there would always be work to do around the place, and didn't she want our kids to be responsible adults? I handed John the scythe and suggested any thistles he didn't cut today would be there tomorrow. For a minute, the boy sagged, then hefted the scythe in his almost-man's hands and headed out the door.

We watched him out the window. As he strode toward the line of dense thistles standing like a wall across the pasture, I explained to Norma that appearances were deceiving.

"That wall of thistles is only about two feet deep. I've been working on the other side. Let's see what he does when he cuts through."

John took his position about half-way along the wall of tough growth where he had left off the day before. He grabbed the scythe by the handles and took a swing at a thin line of thistles; the tough stalks folded at the cut and fell at his feet. He stepped forward and swung again, deeper into the wall, another thin swath. With his third cut he settled into the rhythm a scyther soon develops. Over his shoulder we could see that the dense growth was thinning.

One more swing and he was through into daylight. He stopped and stared. He leaned forward and peered around the standing thistles. Suddenly he understood. The scythe flew up in the air and he danced around in a tight circle of gleeful abandon, a huge smile on his face.

Norma and I hugged each other and laughed with him. John turned toward the window and saw us and did another dance. Then he grabbed up the scythe and swung back into his rhythm, swiftly reducing the rest of the wall to stubble.

The next year I borrowed a neighbor's tractor and sprayer and doused the field with weed-killer—not a good idea. Back in the '60s, herbicides were considered the smart farmer's way to easier crop management, cleaner fields and bigger profits; I just wanted to get ahead of the thistles. I wasn't exactly careless, just your run-of-the-mill part-time homesteader handling the stuff they sell you off the shelves at the co-op.

I poured weed-killer from container to tank, then diluted it with the prescribed amount of water. I didn't use rubber gloves or wear protective clothing. A rain slicker might have kept some of the spray from soaking into my shirt and jeans, and a spray mask would have kept me from inhaling the stuff, but I'd never seen anyone going after thistles on a hot day in June dressed in contamination gear.

So I sprayed the field and spot-sprayed the fence line with a hose. By the time I finished a couple of hours later, I knew I didn't want to do it again. I'd rather scythe thistles for the rest of my life. I tasted that stuff for a week. Most farmers now know there are trade-offs, and handle herbicides and insecticides like the deadly chemicals they are. And avoid them whenever possible, for themselves and for the environment they'll leave to their children.

John Schaefer showed me there was a cheaper and much more realistic alternative. Wait till the thistles begin to bloom, he said, then mow the pasture. Not a perfect answer, since thistles can sprout up again, and there's always thistle seed blowing in from roadside growth—but it beats handling Agent Orange or worse every year. And it does seem to control the weed.

Even amateur farmers like me have a responsibility to the community at large. The choices a farmer makes spread out far beyond his own fences.

NAP TIME

2

Shep and Humility

The small farm we found when we first came to Virginia had all the marks of divine intervention, since we could thank God for a place to rent where there were no others to be found—and blame him/her for the frustrations of living there after we decided to stay in Virginia and bought it. The place accommodated our needs while instructing us in things about ourselves we didn't particularly care to learn, but that's life.

It had twelve acres and an old bank barn, the first thing close to a farm we'd ever lived on. We wound up with two vegetable gardens, some fruit trees, a pony and sixteen sheep, and that was fine with Shep. He was mostly English Shepherd, black with typical markings of tan and white. We didn't know enough about sheep to train him for herding, but his instincts made him their guide and protector.

I think Shep felt he should train *us*. Lesson number one: Shep knew things about sheep we didn't know. And he knew much more about humans than sheep would ever discover. He could bridge our ignorance. Whenever we tried to round up the sheep for worming or shearing, Shep would trot a little ahead, looking back over his shoulder as if to say, "I can get them for you if you'll just tell me which ones you want and where you'd like me to put them."

But rather than listen to his eyes and follow his instincts, I organized the troops instead. After all, how hard could it be to round up sixteen sheep? A neighbor told me the way to do it was to drive the sheep along a fence line into an enclosure or "gate" made of fence wire. Once the sheep were inside, we could close the gate and have the sheep where we could work with them.

"Okay, Norma, you look after the gate and close it when I give you the signal." I wanted to make sure everyone had their responsibilities clearly in mind, no goofing off. Next, I gave our daughters their tasks. "Debby, you and Cathy head out to the right, the boys and I will come in at them from the left." Shep sat down to watch me do his job.

Some say sheep are as stupid as the people who keep them, but our ewes and ram seemed to understand what was needed and cooperated nicely. Jim and John bunched the flock against the fence while the girls flapped their arms to keep them from turning aside. Directly behind the sheep, I filled with pride at how we moved them quickly and cleanly into the enclosure. I congratulated myself. *Not all greenhorns are lacking in common sense.*

I was conscious of a glorious spring day, a deeply blue sky fleeced with soft sheepskin clouds, a gentle breeze fresh with the scent of snowy blossoms hanging from the locusts in the fence row, the children's cheeks aglow with exuberant health, and Norma smiling in admiration as I walked up with the flock, now turned to face me.

"Well, there they are," I boasted.

Just then the ram snorted and started back toward the opening.

I waved my arms. "I guess we better close the gate."

The ram started to trot. I waved and yelled at him, "No

you don't," but he did anyway and broke into a full gallop, hopped twice in the air, hit me in the middle and ran up over my head as I slammed into the ground. I tried to sit up with the flock in flight behind him, and I think sixteen sets of hooves pounded me somewhere, but by then I wasn't counting.

Nearby there was another snort, but it didn't sound like the ram. *I'll roll over in a minute and see what's making the noise,* I thought. At least that was one of the thoughts, but others were more pressing, like *Why can't I breathe? Lord, that ram's heavy. How many feet did he have anyway? I hope he's finished, I sure am. There's that snort again!?*

A breath finally sucked down into my tortured lungs and I managed to roll over. The boys were holding each other up and it was perfectly clear they were *laughing?* I rolled in the other direction to see the girls, Debby on hands and knees, Cathy rolling on the ground beside her. The sound of their indecorous hilarity reached my unbelieving ears.

Surely Norma feels sympathetic. I twisted to see her, but that was where the snorts were coming from. She had her bandanna stuffed in her mouth and was hanging limply from a fence post.

When I rolled back, Shep was there beside me, head cocked, and I felt here was someone who understood my suffering. Except a suspicious grin shaped his face, and the wag of his tail wasn't quite an expression of sympathy, it seemed to me.

If I could understand his non-verbal language, he was saying, "Next time leave it to me, okay?" I had a lot to learn about so much; why did it take so long to learn it?

* * *

"Blessed are the poor in spirit, for theirs is the kingdom of heaven." This first of his Beatitudes is one of the more confusing things Jesus said to the people who gathered to hear him. It wasn't the shape of his statement that was unusual; to begin a new proverb with "Blessed are…" goes back in Israel's history to Moses and Joshua and David. But poor in spirit did not mesh either with common concepts of righteousness then nor with our ideas of personal identity and self-esteem now. Who wants to be thought of as poor in spirit? Sounds humiliating, like you're on the bottom of the totem pole, with the rest of the world standing on your head.

Yet the first thing Jesus says to the crowd around him is that it's okay to admit to yourself that you feel under the pile, aren't getting anywhere, don't know where you're going. You've made mistakes and sometimes feel next to worthless. You are definitely not in control of your life. When you're that poor in spirit, Jesus says, you're not just close to the kingdom of God, it's yours to move into, with all the contentment and happiness being poor in spirit could never find before.

* * *

Under the layers of religious impulse we've built up around Jesus, his basic message is often buried: *we are called to be transformed from what we are into a new creation.* It's a mysterious process of change not covered by words like education or maturation or biological evolution. Helpful as these concepts are, they don't come close to explaining what goes on in the course of an "awakening" life.

Isn't it odd? We live at first as if there is not much more to add to what we already understand about life, simply because we have reached a level of competence in living. We do what we do and it seems enough. Yet there comes a day—if we aren't stone hardened inside—when we see ourselves against a better, larger reality, one full of light and integrity and mercy. Jesus painted word pictures about this reality again and again, trying to separate it from the religious plaster people always pile on to thoughts about God.

It takes humility to discover there is much more to life than our everyday reality, which is why our everyday reality looks the way it does. So there's nothing wrong with humility, and being on the bottom of the pile, because there's not so much to unload from our lives before we begin the transformation of mind and spirit and being that Jesus called a new birth. Humiliation is just a wake-up call, although the experiences can be hard to swallow at the time.

Like being run over by a flock of sheep; while it's a humiliation you'd not want to repeat, it holds the potential for new understandings. Sometimes humiliation can become a profound educational experience, moving us toward a new integrity in a greater reality.

Even if it seems like a dog's life at first.

* * *

Shep's personal humiliation gave us all a new experience in a wider reality. He holds a reasonable respect for skunks; I've heard tell of dogs with more curiosity than brains who will tackle anything that moves, including skunks. But not Shep.

Sheppy knew a lot of things instinctively. I like to think instincts mean you know about something without having to study on it, like sex. Yet like most people, and some dogs, knowing about something didn't always protect Shep. Especially when he met a skunk face to face in the dark one night just outside the back door of our next home in Virginia, a big old farm house we rented after a brief return to Canada in 1970.

The problem for Shep was that he possessed another instinct. Like a mother protects her child, a dog worth his keep will defend his home. That's why Shep urinated on the fence at the back of the lot, the tree at the corner, and the utility pole out by the road. Other dogs took note of his new territory. But a skunk doesn't pay attention to marked territories.

That night Shep was caught off guard by two bright little eyes shining at him in the dark. The eyes reflected the porch light, yet the bare bulb wasn't bright enough to show Sheppy who or what crouched behind them.

Then the light in the eyes went out. It's one thing to be surprised by eyes staring back at you out of the night, quite another by eyes that suddenly are *not* staring at you. Particularly if you haven't figured out who they belong to. Poor Shep. He leaped for where the eyes had been, his instinct to protect his home stronger than his desire to know first what was there.

The eyes disappeared when the skunk turned so his anal glands and sprayer, just under his tail, were in position for defense, a very smart move for the skunk. Because skunks turn away from a fight, some people think they're stupid. Skunks seem laughable as they snuffle along with noses to the ground, not seeming to notice what's going on around them.

While Sheppy laughed a lot, he never laughed at skunks. He laughed when he chased a stick someone would throw for him. He laughed whenever anyone suggested going for a walk. And he smiled in his eyes as he sat on the hill beside our house and watched a sunset. We saw him do this often and wondered what a sky of such iridescence meant to him.

But Shep wasn't smiling now. When he leaped at where the eyes had been, he found out whose they were. Too late. A jet of oily yellow liquid hit Sheppy on his chest and neck. Then as his weight lifted the skunk off his feet, Shep took some more spray in his face.

There's not much a dog can do in such a situation. It's not like bumping into someone on the street when you say you're sorry and help them pick up their groceries. Not like that at all. You may be very sorry, but with a skunk you leave first and think of apologies later. And you can't leave fast enough.

An overwhelming smell drifted into the house. Skunk spray is like that, strong and penetrating. I think even if you lived in inch-thick plastic, it would take only moments longer for an angry skunk to let you know he's around.

We have noticed on other occasions the accidental demise of a skunk on the highway over the hill. As swiftly as life is squashed by a car, it is not swift enough; even in death the skunk achieves a whiff of victory. But this night was not one of those distant highway disasters. Not at all. There was an instant relevance and vigor to this odor which suggested a more localized occasion. Like out in the back yard.

"Where's Shep?" someone yelled. Cathy opened the back door and closed it again, but not quickly enough. Shep nearly knocked her over in his haste to escape his learning experience. Since one shot of skunk spray had taken him full in the face, his eyes were half-closed and watering, and the spray couldn't have tasted any better than it smelled because he was foaming at the mouth.

In spite of the skunk spray, Cathy grabbed Shep by the collar as he stumbled blindly past her. She may be the baby of the family, but she's tough.

"He's *really* been skunked," she yelled, a fact now obvious to everyone else in the house. The white fur on his chest showed a dirty yellow stain, his mouth poured saliva and his eyes wept a stream of tears. Shep lurched along, pawing at his face as Cathy steered him through the dining room toward the front door and away from the skunk out back.

Cathy threw open the door and Shep plunged gratefully into the fresh air, down the steps and onto the lawn. He rolled on his back and rubbed his head and eyes on the grass, wiping them back and forth fiercely. Then he whipped over onto his stomach and, shoving with his hind legs, he plowed along on his chest, trying to erase the skunk's oily spray.

The taste must have been terrible because he would stop and paw at his mouth, then roll again on the grass or plow his way around the yard. Finally he crawled under the fence and disappeared into the dark, racing for the creek and a drink.

No one saw Sheppy for two days. Just about the time the house began to lose the worst of its smell, he came back. He was dusty from scrubbing himself on the ground, and he still smelled richly of skunk, but he had rid himself of the worst of the gummy spray. And he was very hungry.

There's not much to do for a friend who has been skunked, except wash him down with tomato juice. And rinse him with water. The acid in the tomato juice lifts the oily spray, at least it's supposed to. Then it all has to be rinsed away, and for a dog who prefers to take his own bath, Sheppy found it hard to take.

Sometimes it takes all the help we can stand to get the smell out of our lives.

GROUNDHOG

3

Snake Shock and Groundhog Gardening

It has been said that if you sit on a hot stove, you will prove Einstein's theory of relativity: time stands still while mass turns into steaming energy. But no one I've met has ever sat on a hot stove willingly or acknowledged the practice, so the value of this simple experiment remains in doubt. I have been known to lean against one inadvertently, but not in the nature of an experiment and I can assure you it is not worth replication, unless you're pushed to it.

There are other situations more suited to turning time inside out. If you sit down on a porch swing on a steaming summer's eve and the wisteria vine beside your head slithers, even if it's just a black snake trying to get away, you will experience snake shock. Guaranteed. I suspect there are snake handlers who will chuckle and tell us not to be frightened: "Why, that's just a friendly four-foot rat snake, sometimes known as a pilot black snake; he's more afraid of you than you are of him."

No he isn't. In a moment or two, time may catch up to itself once more, space may move beyond the wisteria and the swing, and I may breathe again, all things being relative. Snake shock. And Frog Hollow has its snakes.

One day I was scything some grass for the horses when I saw it–a garter snake, about a foot long. It was a good thing I was on the backswing or I might have lost a leg. Snake shock anywhere is a shattering experience, and the size or variety of the snake has nothing to do with it.

There he was, strung out on the branches of the tall grass, slithering through the tops of his "trees." We both stopped and stared at each other. He was light enough and the grass was tough enough that it barely moved as he placed his weight on a leaf branch. Perhaps some primordial memory reminded him of his tropical cousins, the constrictors, and their life in the trees of the jungle. Or maybe he was just catching some bugs.

Those big, long black snakes are good to have around a garden. They will even help keep the rodent population under control. Because anywhere a mouse can go, so can a black snake. And they have big appetites.

Our first place in the Valley had an old chicken house occupied by some bantams left by the previous owners. They were as independent as banties usually are, so we never got close to them, yet the hens still used the nesting boxes.

Chopping some thistles nearby one Saturday, I heard a banty fussing itself in the chicken house. So I looked in the window. A four foot long black snake had hoisted himself up into the nesting boxes and was having some eggs for breakfast while the hen watched in consternation.

I ran to get the children to come see, but I could have walked, because he was hungry and had a mind to get himself around a few breakfasts while the supply lasted.

He nudged an egg lengthwise, then started to stretch his mouth around it. If you've ever mended a small sock over a big lightbulb, you'll know how he looked. To get more stretch, he unhinged his jaw as he worked the egg back into his throat.

"Now what will he do?" Debby asked, as the bulge of the egg made the snake look grossly uncomfortable.

"Watch," John cautioned. Suddenly the snake contorted, like throwing a loop down a garden hose; he crushed the eggshell and the bulge was gone.

As I said, snakes can get in anywhere. I picked up the telephone to make a call one day, looked down to dial and nearly swallowed the mouthpiece. On the floor at my feet lay a two-foot-long blacksnake with its tail emerging from under the bookcase.

If I hadn't found him then, he might have disappeared up the vacuum hose when Norma cleaned the room that morning. That is if she didn't see him first and go out the window.

He may have been the same snake Cathy found under a hay bale on the back porch. A scream from her brought us all thundering out to where she was now leaning on the bale to recover. Everybody shouted for a moment and then she got her message across. "Snake. Snake underneath—" she gasped, pointing under the bale.

The snake was probably as shocked as Cathy was, particularly when she dropped the bale back on him. Probably Cathy would have hollered at anything she found moving under that bale, but a snake didn't even have to move to startle her.

Snake shock. How come most of us react like that? I mind the time Debby found a little gartersnake when we were still in Ontario. She was just a little girl then and didn't know to be frightened. The boys and I were fixing a shed roof while Norma's father sat behind it in the shade. We could see her coming to show us, but Grandpa couldn't. She ran up on her five-year-old legs, waving the snake in front of her. We admired from the roof, so she kept on going, round back to show Grandpa.

When Grandpa recovered, he was half-way over the fence

into the neighbor's field. So I wasn't too ashamed of my snake shock experiences.

* * *

Shep taught us something about fancy gardening. Anyone who has ever gardened knows the temptation to try new ways of doing old things. Like growing tomatoes. If there's a way to torture tomato plants, we've probably tried it. Trenching. Staking. Tying the growing shoots to fence wire or to twine stretched between posts. Each time, we give up and go back to the lazy man's method; let the boogers sprawl out on hay mulch and forget the tying and pruning, just pick as they ripen and be grateful.

The temptations arise during the off season, when dream gardens are designed and never a bug infests or a back kinks. Reading about gardening fits the dream mold too; the gardens of magazines never really exist except in the fabulous imaginations of an editor and an ever-creative photographer. I don't know how the tomatoes in those pictures achieve their color or size, but that's part of the off-season game.

In one of those magazine articles, someone with cantaloupe-sized tomatoes swore the secret lay in growing them on raised platforms of chicken wire and gave precise details of this most advanced method of horticulture. Easy-to-follow instructions showed how to construct the platforms in a few minutes, and right there, any sensible garden dreamer would have put away his bubble-pipe and come to his senses. Not me. I fall for stuff like that.

That spring, following his plan, I drove stakes into the soil along both sides of the row of young tomato plants and joined the stakes with 1x2 boards to make a sturdy frame about 18 inches off the ground. Then Norma and I stretched a roll of 36-inch chicken wire along the frame and stapled it fast to the boards. Easy enough, and it only took about twice as long as it did for the dreamer in the article. Maybe he didn't count how long it took to sharpen the posts or take the kinks out of the wire, but then it was his dream, not ours.

After that, all the gardener has to do is wait for the tomato plant to grow up to the wire, at which point he guides it through the mesh and lets it flourish abundantly on top. The dreamer claims the benefits are numerous — no ground rot, lots of air circulation to promote ripening, no slugs, reduced rodent damage, and much easier to prune and harvest. How could we lose?

But the tomato plants never got the message. We did what we were supposed to do, pushed the main stalks through the wire and pruned back all the other growth we could see and reach, but we were fighting the inevitable. On hands and elbows, it was grope time in the underbrush, and in the shade of the upper growth we missed a number of shoots which soon led to a wild profusion of pale yellow leaves underneath. Up top, new growth kept trying to dive back under the wire. We poked the drooping shoots back up through and wove them in so they'd stay, but it was a pain in the knees and sciatic nerves, to say the least.

Green tomatoes began to show themselves in mid-July, most of them hanging under the wire where their weight had pulled them down and where they'd never see the sun to ripen. How did the dreamer manage to defy gravity and get his tomatoes to stay on top until they were big enough not to fall through the wire? We pulled the small tomatoes up top again, hung them over branches and rested them on leaf clumps bigger than the openings in the wire, but it was a balancing act, and some fell back through if we jiggled the wire at all. And how do you grope around underneath, poking small tomatoes up through, without jiggling the wire?

It might have worked, even with all that extraneous screwing around, if it hadn't been for the groundhog. I had not yet built a fence around the garden, so he had it all to himself; but he was taking a considerable risk because Shep patrolled the yard just beyond the tomato row. In the early light of morning, I could see where the varmint had grazed on our beans, but I didn't expect him to be still in the garden.

Groundhogs are wary animals and don't like to be caught in the open. That morning as I rounded the potato rows, he looked up at me, his mouth full of juicy Oak Leaf lettuce. When I yelled, Shep took a leap from his doze in the grass, and the groundhog scuttled for the tomato patch and dove under the netting, Shep no more than a jawsnap behind.

I yelled again and Norma arrived, huffing a question. "Whatsa matter?"

I pointed as Shep tried to squeeze his hind end under the 1x2, pitching soil in great gouts behind him. He finally flipped his right haunch under his left and disappeared underneath like he was swimming the side stroke. The groundhog pushed in deeper. We could see his progress in the tomato plants up top; they wriggled as he passed underneath. Shep must have got both his back feet under him again because the wire screening humped up as he plunged in pursuit.

"Look at what he's doing," Norma yelped. "Shep, come here! Come here NOW!" she roared, but he wasn't about to quit the chase, not as close as he was to the back end of the woodchuck.

The woodchuck zigged toward daylight, looked out and saw us getting closer and zagged back toward the middle of the patch. Shep thundered on, pulling tomato stalks back through the chickenwire, stripping green tomatoes off like pearls from a broken necklace. He zigged after his prey and zagged even quicker to close the gap. A steady stream of canine invective—enraged yelps, smothered gasping barks and squeals—rose above the tearing sound of our tomatoes being destroyed as the two animals ripped through the vines.

If the groundhog had taken the short route *across* the

row, maybe a few plants would have survived, but he'd gone in at the end of the row and didn't leave until he got to the other end, with Shep right on his tail. The woodchuck shot up over the farm fence on the north side of our garden and I thought maybe Shep would make it too, but he draws the line at climbing fences. He scuffled the ground at the bottom of the wire for a moment but saw it was buried and raced away to the fence gate he knew he could squeeze under. By the time he got back on the trail, the groundhog had made it safely to his hole under the Seckle pear tree in the orchard.

So ended the lesson. We ripped up the netting and bought our tomatoes at the market in town. Shep knew it was a stupid idea to begin with.

*   *   *

Life has a way of tearing up our tomatoes. Surprises—not good ones—catch us off-balance. Faith needs its exercise to grow more resilient, more capable of dealing with life's twists and turns. We could turn to Saturday's farmers' market for some tomatoes, but Shep faced an immediate twist, with no time to consider options. He had a groundhog to catch.

It's pleasant to have a rose-colored view of reality. Time to think, to relax and pray about our options. But only as long as we can accept the surprises when they come.

BLACKBERRIES

4

The Price of Integrity

At last count we've lived in twenty-three homes since we've been married. Some places we did not live in for very long: my brother's place for a week, just after the honeymoon (not recommended). An old apartment building in the days when summer "air- conditioning" meant sitting up on 100 degree nights holding the baby in the meager breeze through the hall door. Winnipeg can be a furnace in August.

Over the years we learned more than we wanted to about moving and housing and renting and losing your shirt. But we were very much a part of the times—job transfers, education, new opportunities. Abraham moved by faith and camels, we moved by hope and a rental van. And wound up in the Shenandoah Valley.

After finishing my degree in the spring semester of 1964 at Eastern Mennonite University, I was offered a job locally as a staff writer with Mennonite Broadcasts (now Mennonite Media Ministries), work I found rewarding and demanding. Except for the staff meetings.

Over the next few years, we kept wondering when

we'd be moving back. Canada was home, with a different temperament, a different sense of purpose. Since we'd never actually said to ourselves, "Let's emigrate," but rather, "Let's go away to finish Jim's education," we wondered if we should resume our lives in the country of our birth. But Sheppy knew something that had escaped us—he had taken us as his country, a matter of belonging wherever we happened to live. So when the five-year waiting period expired, we began the process of becoming American citizens. And I started my own business as a free-lance writer—still looking for Place, I suspect, still reaching out for the Reality of God beyond the ordinary lives we were living.

* * *

We were church people now, twice on Sunday, once midweek plus committees. Yet somehow, in spite of the sincerity of our motives, the busyness of religious life obscured and even interfered with the intricate process of evolving into the image of God. As Jesus pointed out to the Pharisees, their religion had taken on a life of its own and blocked their way to Reality. Yet he didn't make it any easier for the crowd of ordinary listeners, telling them their righteousness must exceed that of the Pharisees!? So how do you live with religion without getting swallowed up by it? Is the alternative to ignore the church and live as if the spirit and presence of God no longer matters?

There's a common flaw in both approaches to life, no matter how expedient each may seem at the time. We get so thoroughly wrapped up in our religion—or our irreligion—that we cannot hear the Voice. Without the Voice there's no Face and reality has no recognizable dimension but what we give to it ourselves. Like looking in a mirror. We're captured by the culture we've created, and cannot or will not take part in our own transformation, the calling to move into and inhabit the image of God.

*   *   *

We sold the first place we owned in Virginia, and eventually bought land in the hollow. The spring and summer of 1972, when we built our version of a mountain house, Norma became a contractor in addition to all her other job descriptions. We planned the house and ordered the materials, hired the crews and intended to do as much of the work as we could ourselves. We were going to build it together, but then I was asked to write a series of six video pieces on examples of good public education in Virginia.

So while I breezed around the state interviewing students and teachers, Norma ran errands for the carpenters, hauled lumber and nails and a hundred other kinds of materials in our old pickup, and settled territorial squabbles between the electrician and the plumber. And if she'd been about four inches taller, she'd have caught the scam of the concrete block crew. I didn't do much to help her that spring, but I did find out something was wrong with our basement, and got a lump on my head in the process.

When I came home that weekend, the walkout basement was laid up and the house roughed in above. It was a busy year in construction, and though we managed to hire carpenters from the area, the masonry crew drove in from Winchester, about 70 miles down the valley.

"The carpenters want to install the windows next week," Norma said as she led me around to the basement door. "But Friday afternoon they uncrated the front window for the basement. Joe Sawyer tried it in the wall opening and it didn't fit."

She stepped over the doorsill and I followed, and whacked my head on the cement lintel across the top of the doorway. Stunned for a moment, I couldn't understand why I'd grown so much that I would need to duck my head. I walked back to the doorway again and gingerly tried to walk through.

"This doorway isn't tall enough," I muttered, "but why?" We stood and peered at the doorway, and the wall above it. A terrible thought lifted itself into both of our minds at the same time.

I said it for both of us: "They've left out a course of block!"

Norma had a tape rule in her pocket and we measured the wall height; it was eight inches shorter than it should have been. Then she measured the window opening—again short a block. "That's why the window won't fit," she said quietly, putting her hands to her head as if to hold it on. "But we can't lift the house up now." There was a quiver in her voice.

She spun around and looked at the other window openings. "They'll all be too small! None of the windows will fit!"

We spent the rest of the morning going over the walls and the blueprints. Not only had the crew left out a course of cement block, but they'd put two window openings in the wrong places, where partitions were supposed to go for room dividers. Of the ten openings in the basement, nine were wrong. In two other places, broken blocks stared back at us like missing teeth, gaps in a wall meant to be solid. We stared at each other.

"I suppose we can live with a lower ceiling," I suggested. "Maybe we can get them to dig out some more clay and lower the floor a little to help."

Norma smiled slowly. "I've only paid the first half of their contract. They still have to put in the retaining walls outside and seal the block."

So we wrote out a detailed list of the mistakes, marking them on the blueprints. I hung around long enough on Monday to talk to the crew chief.

He didn't even apologize. He told us to take back the windows and get smaller ones. What about the openings where partitions were called for, I asked. Move the partitions, he replied. And the holes from broken blocks? He'd patch them.

Norma reminded him he had not been paid in full, and that we'd use the money for the balance of the contract to repair the damage. He started to get mean.

Behind him—and listening—stood Joe Sawyer, the carpenter, with one of his helpers. Joe walked up beside the block man and beckoned to his helper to come too. Joe, a wiry little man, had a pry bar in his hand.

"Jim," he said, "I know a mason who'd help you straighten out this mess." The block man muttered something, and Joe tapped him on the arm with the pry bar. "You said you didn't want to fix your mistakes, so you got no complaint."

Joe turned to us. "While he leaves, maybe we could talk about the siding. If you still want the barn board, I figured out how much I'll need." We walked over to his truck. I turned to see the block man staring after us, standing where we had left him.

Joe smiled and nodded toward the man. "Don't worry about him. We've seen his kind a few times. He was in too much of a hurry to do the job right. And his help played the fool most of the time. He won't last. Thank God for that."

Maybe Joe was right, and he wouldn't last. In the world of boards, block and bumped heads, it helps to think the laws of the marketplace will catch up to an indifferent workman and put him out of business. Business reality may not look much like God's reality sometimes, but honesty always gives evidence of itself.

* * *

Looking back, it was the integrity and honesty of Joe Sawyer that kept us from hardened attitudes of cynicism and suspicion. Over the months that followed, we began to understand that in the hollow, honesty and personal integrity are considered priceless assets. It was to be our first lesson: Integrity is more important to our neighbors than anyone's formal belief. Honest dealings give the most reliable evidence of the unseen God and his purpose for our lives.

The confrontation between Joe and the chief of the block-laying crew made it clear that we could still trust some people. The quality of life among our neighbors soon demonstrated which ones were worthy of trust; they had been working at it for awhile.

In one way or another, without exception, the lives worth trusting had paid dearly for their integrity.

* * *

Irvin Hottinger now drives an East/West Fuel Oil truck, but he didn't stop by our place to deliver oil Saturday; he had his dog and his berry pail instead. We had met the day before at the Co-op. Irvin was buying some ten-penny nails. I was giving the clerk my address for a repair order on my chain saw, and Irv asked where that was in the hollow. When I told him where we'd built our house last year, he got a far away look in his eye and a little smile twitched at the corner of his mouth.

"You pick any blackberries on that hill?" he asked. A squiggle of greying hair poked through above the adjusting strap on his company bill cap. He tipped the cap back and his brown eyes gleamed with the question.

Stuffing the repair ticket in a pocket, I nodded. "It's a real good year. My wife's canned 30 quarts of blackberries and 20 some pints of jam already. You know the hill, Irvin?" But I didn't need to ask. He was picking imaginary blackberries out of the air and putting them in his mouth.

"Best blackberries I ever ate," he murmured reverently. "That patch at the top by the big cherry tree still there?"

"Yep," I replied. "Good patch of wineberries grows right beside them, but they're almost finished for the year."

Irvin put the bag of nails and a twenty on the counter. "My Grandpa Cloyd Hottinger owned the farm across the hill when I was a boy; I spent most of my summers on the place." The clerk gave him his change and put the register slip in the bag. "House is still there, that old yellow one by the creek, with the chickenhouse falling down. Barn's gone though."

"Used to play in the barn. Broke my arm there." He took the bag and we walked toward the door. "Grandma Daisy told me after I got better it was the best accident she never hoped to see."

He looked at me to see if I'd take the bait. He'd fished with that worm before, and I bit. "She what?"

"Best accident she never hoped to see again, she said." Irvin chuckled as I turned around and sat on the edge of a counter. He'd seen biters like me hooked before, too.

"I tripped over a doorsill beam following Daisy out to where the milk cans were cooling in the spring house. Snapped one of my forearm bones. Daisy hated that doorsill and wanted Cloyd to cut it out. Wasn't a week went by she didn't hit that thing with a full pail of milk and lose some."

"A pail of milk's heavy, weighs about half as much as she did, at least that's what she told Cloyd. That always got a laugh out of Cloyd because Daisy was as round as she was tall. Her trouble was she couldn't have been over five foot high, and the beam sat up a good foot. She had to hoist the pail up and over; if she didn't clip that beam coming up, she'd hit it going down the other side."

"Either way she'd spill some milk, and she'd remind Cloyd it wasn't all that easy getting milk in the pail in the first place. She could remind good."

Irvin settled against the counter beside me and took breath. "But Cloyd's father had built the barn himself, hewed every beam by hand, and Cloyd just didn't feel comfortable cutting through a beam his daddy had laid, even if he'd tripped over the thing himself enough to cuss it out."

Irvin reached into his East/West jacket, pulled out a pouch of Red Man chewing tobacco and began to pluck himself a cheekful. "After I busted my arm, Daisy told Cloyd to get rid of that beam or she would. She wasn't going to see anyone else break a bone because of it. Cloyd felt bad about me getting hurt, and he would have cut it out right then, but he took a fancy to the idea of Daisy doing something about it herself."

He tucked the chaw into his mouth and put away the pouch. "So Cloyd let it go. I think he wanted to see what Daisy would do."

"Daisy waited about two weeks, and she got more upset every day, but he'd just smile at her and wink at me. Then one day when Cloyd was loading a couple calves for the stock sale, Daisy hoisted a pail of milk over the beam and the edge tipped the pail on the way down and she lost about a quart. I never knew Daisy to swear, but she sat down on the beam and started to damn the beam and Cloyd and his father and the milk pail too. She got up again and took a wild kick at the pail, but it was still pretty full and solid and she had old running shoes on, so she hurt her big toe bad, and that made her madder, so she took to yelling for Cloyd as she limped out the door of the barn."

Irvin's head swung around as he looked for somewhere to spit. Behind the counter he found a garbage pail; he pitched his chin toward it and loosed a brown splat onto the plastic liner.

He took a fresh grip on his story. "Daisy hollered for Cloyd to come cut out that fool beam, but Cloyd and his truck were out the lane and heading for town. I watched from the barn as Daisy circled in the barn driveway, so riled she could bite. Then she got herself together and went over to the shop. I could hear her talking to herself and making noises like she was pitching tools on the floor looking for something."

"In a minute Daisy came hustling out the shop door with a buck saw in her hand; it looked as big as her. She ran into the barn past me and got down on her knees in front of the beam and started chewing at it with the saw. She pushed and pulled it across the beam until it settled into one of the notches she'd half started."

Irvin hoisted himself up onto the counter as much to rest his breath as his bones. "Daisy's face got redder as she hauled on the saw. Cutting a beam with a buck saw's hard work even for a logger, and that beam was locust wood, tough as a pig's nose. Daisy'd get to sawing about a half dozen strokes, then she'd stop and rest herself on her heels. But only for a little, then she'd grab the saw and go back at it again."

"She'd be there yet if Doc Williamson, the vet, hadn't stopped by to pick up a drenching tube he'd left in the barn on his last call. When he saw Daisy gnawing away at that beam, he crowed like a rooster and climbed over to grab the other end of the saw."

"'I've been after Cloyd for years to get shut of this thing,' Doc told Daisy. 'I've tripped over it for the last time.' Doc's a big man and strong, he was making the sawdust fly and Daisy looked as if she was hanging on more than helping. It didn't take long till they cut through to the spongy rot near the bottom."

"Daisy would have kept on cutting, but Doc stopped and pulled the saw out and started on the other side. He laughed and said he'd give a day's work to see Cloyd's face the first time he walks through. 'I bet he trips on what's gone, I bet he does.'"

"But Cloyd didn't get home till evening and Doc was gone, taking the cut-out piece of beam with him. He said he didn't want Cloyd trying to glue it back. And Cloyd must have felt bad leaving Daisy with the beam still there, because he brought her a Baby Ruth bar, her favorite, and a new flyswatter."

Irvin slid off the counter, so I got down too, and we started toward the door again. Family loyalty reaches out beyond the years; I could see Irvin wanted to say something more about Cloyd and his respect for Daisy's patience over the years.

"Cloyd never said a word to Daisy about the beam, and Doc never mentioned he'd been the one to cut it out, with Daisy's help. Cloyd thought Daisy did it herself, and after a time he got to bragging on her. Had a big laugh at himself when he found out what really happened."

*   *   *

Irvin's experience with doorways brought him a broken arm, not a bump on the head like mine. And his grandmother renewed her bruised integrity through decisive action.

According to the Gospel of Matthew, the next proverb-beatitude Jesus gave the crowd ran something like, "Fortunate are you who mourn, for you will be comforted." Daisy grieved for her grandson Irvin's pain and anguish; she blamed herself bitterly for the accident and the needless injury the child suffered. She should have insisted her husband cut out the problem long ago, but she hadn't done so. She sucked up the responsibility, and it drove her to action.

*   *   *

Irvin climbed into his pickup, a blue Ford F150 with a battered white toolbox behind the cab. A big redbone hound sat on the seat beside him, nose out the passenger-side window. Irvin cranked down his window. "You know, Jim, the year he died, Cloyd and Daisy had their sixtieth anniversary. She didn't last but a couple months after, said he'd be too lonely without her. I believe she was right."

Irvin stuck the key in the ignition; I put a hand on his window, then leaned in so he could hear me. "Bring your hound and come pick some berries. You know where they are."

Irvin smiled. "Since you got enough, don't mind if I do."

"COWS"

5

Identity and Illusion

Our neighbor Ivy Moyers will need galoshes to get out through the dew to milk her cow this morning. Ivy's land lies across the road from ours. Stooped and frail, her white hair swathed in a scarf, Ivy may weigh 100 pounds fully dressed—and that's including a wool sweater and the old raincoat she wears outdoors. It's a brisk October morning in the hollow, and a fire feels good in the kitchen stove.

Little North Mountain is clothed in lumpen folds of fog. The eaves are dripping, but quietly, all sound softened by the moisture-laden air. A soggy breeze wobbles the leaves on the black locusts. Sun-browned orchard grass is slick underfoot.

A Holstein doesn't take the day off in bad weather. When a cow is in milk, you've got to milk her twice a day, rain or shine, for better or worse until she dries up. If Ivy missed milking her mostly-white Holstein, Tansy, this morning, the cow would come get her by midday.

Mrs. Moyers and Tansy have an understanding. If it is reasonable weather and the cow is up in the pasture, it makes sense to disturb things as little as possible. A more regulated homesteader would stable the cow, put its pail-knocking head in a stanchion, tie its head-swatting tail to a post, and bring in the wheelbarrow and shovel for the manure.

Now, that seems a lot of anxiety just for a pail of milk, so Mrs. Moyers and her cow have worked out an arrangement. If Tansy stands nicely for milking right where she is in the pasture, all the fussing with stanchions and ropes and wheelbarrows can be dispensed with. It saves Ivy half an hour of barn chores. It saves the cow a lot of walking, and she doesn't miss any grazing time.

Mind you, a heavy dew or a skin of snow can make climbing the hill to the pasture a problem, even more so coming down the hill with a pail of milk. But Ivy and Tansy may have worked up a deal on that, too. If Ivy takes a little longer over breakfast and maybe has another cup of coffee, Tansy will get the message and come meet her at the gate.

Ivy lives alone. Her children are grown and married with children of their own, but they never leave her alone for too long. Every Sunday they come to visit, maybe play ball in the pasture, and Ivy is the center of her family again. Through the week she talks to them on the telephone (blessed invention), and they check up on her when she's feeling poorly.

But they don't bother to call her at milking time. She and Tansy are busy.

* * *

"Too many people think happiness means having everything they want," Ivy Moyers said one day as we sat by her Warm Morning stove, trying to get some January out of our bones.

Ivy and her husband had struggled through the worst part of the Depression on the meager wages a farm laborer might make in a 14–hour day. She had mended clothes with old pieces of cotton until only the mends remained. She had planted a garden with seeds saved from last year's crop, and somehow she and her family had survived. She doesn't like to remember the details; between God and good neighbors, they got by. Ivy still loves sweet potatoes, a root her family lived on through many a late spring until a new garden could produce.

"If it weren't for sweet potatoes, rutabagas and cabbage, I don't know how people could have lived back in those days," Ivy said. In April when wild asparagus began to send up shoots along the road and dandelions started to grow on the sunny side of the chicken house, she would have some fresh greens to add to their diet.

"Nowadays," Ivy told us, "most people don't know where to look for greens or how to tell a mushroom from a toadstool." Norma nodded and looked sideways at me before she replied, "Ivy, we've only eaten morels. I wouldn't feel safe eating any other wild mushroom—too many of them are poisonous."

"See?" Ivy figured we had just reinforced her point of view. She knew Norma and I were culturally deprived youngsters who had lost touch with the real stuff of existence.

In the spring, Ivy looked for dandelion greens. Imagine how good they must have tasted to someone who hadn't had a feed of fresh vegetables for a couple of months. We're spoiled by California spinach and asparagus from Peru; we can buy lettuce at the supermarket all year long. It's so easy to pick up a package of greens along with the milk and bread and a video at the mall. One-stop shopping for basics and culture—if we can afford it.

* * *

Norma figures that for most women now, homesteading and homemaking are for the chosen. Maybe they always were.

Has it become culturally impractical for a woman to be

a homestead-homemaker? As many as eighty women out of a hundred work outside of the home now, some enjoying a satisfying career, but most (like most men) doing a job that's just a paycheck at the end of the week. Reality for them isn't personal fulfillment in a satisfying career. For every woman who works at a career she has chosen for herself, there must be a hundred working for survival.

When our kids were growing up, Norma planted a garden every spring, kept a freezer full of food and a cold room stocked with over 500 quarts of vegetables, fruit, jams, and pickles, baked all our bread, churned butter, made dresses for our girls, did all my typing until she could teach me how, took our kids to the library every week, read them stories, helped them with their homework, chauffeured them until they got their own driver's licenses, and listened with unfeigned interest to all our dreams plus the sorrows of women friends who found her sympathy something they could lean on.

Yet when someone asks her, "What do you do?" they don't want to hear of the rich significance of her life in those terms. They want her to declare her achievements—or at least find her identity—in the world of business and the professions, the "real" world.

Doing what others expect you to do gets in the way of living out your inner convictions. People are different, but they'd better not be too different. We haven't learned to accept the right of someone else to hold another point of view. What's real for one may not be the same for another, yet we expect others to think or act or believe as we do—especially in terms of religion.

It's a wonder anyone cares to believe in anything. But how we treat each other's beliefs doesn't change God and his reality. Love doesn't change its nature or its power. Forgiveness is the same in any language, any creed. Compassion leaps national and ethnic boundaries. Humility doesn't depend on muscle and firepower. And integrity rises to its strength through our faith in God.

* * *

Ivy has never worried about her role in life. She knows who she is and why she's here. Existential confusion and identity crises may be widespread sources of modern angst, but Ivy lived through the Depression instead.

She has heard that some people think religion—meaning her religion, too?—is just a superstition, and prayer a rabbit's foot to rub for good luck. She snorts at the idea, and her faded blue eyes snap with indignation. She can't prove anything about God to anyone who hasn't lived through the life she has lived, but that's their problem, not hers.

Ivy raised seven children to be honest, kindly, hard-working people with their own children and grandchildren. She accomplished some of this as a widow in a small five-room house with no central heat, no bathroom, and no running water. This was her reality at work, and it focused her faith in God. Or to turn it around, this was her God at work, and it focused her faith in reality.

For Ivy the beloved Face has a name—Jesus. Here was a life she understood. Jesus had no time for unrealities: religious posturing, one-upsmanship, the complaints of the well-to-do. He gave the poor respect, asking no more than what they could give: honesty, forgiveness, compassion, and the will to follow his Father's leading. No matter what others might think of her faith, Jesus gave Ivy the dignity to be her own person. She in turn gave him her undivided loyalty. His spirit was her counselor, her advocate in the courts of heaven. Ivy had no problem with her situation; she had an integrity of being that had nothing to do with her circumstances but everything to do with the presence of God in her life.

Blessed are the meek, for they will inherit the earth.

* * *

Our dog Shep knew something of Ivy's approach to life; he knew how to be himself. Although he lived virtually all his years with humans, he took delight in being his own dog within the constraints such a life imposed. Like many of our country neighbors, we didn't keep our dog on a chain or in a pen, so he enjoyed considerable freedom. His respect for the territorial rights of others kept him from wandering more than was necessary for adventure. The odd time that other dogs came by, he would rub noses and explore anatomies like a good host, then see to it they moved along after a suitable visit. In the meantime he lived in the circle of our family, content to share life's incongruities with us. Like Ivy Moyers' new cow, he used his opportunities to make life more entertaining. Nobody pushed him into a different identity; he chose to discover and explore his own.

Ivy found the new cow in her pasture one morning. Strange circumstance. And strange cow, since it won't milk. And it can't lay eggs either. What with taxes the way they are and the price of coal going up, Ivy needs livestock that can produce, not another freeloader on the place.

But at least this new cow is no longer a horse. It changed when it moved across the road from David Reedy's farm.

Like most in the hollow, David Reedy is a part-time farmer and a full-time something else. In his day job, he's a heavy equipment operator, driving a front-end loader for a paving contractor.

David's big white-feathered gander had been a horse on his place for awhile; the only other white thing the gander could identify with was David's 20-year-old mare, a pink-eyed albino walking horse.

The albino mare is David Reedy's pride and joy. Even though he and the mare are getting long in the tooth, they still go for a ride occasionally, when it's warm. By the time they bend by our lane, stiff bones have loosened and unwary muscles have yet to tighten for both of them. So David is riding tall and the mare is swinging along in that easy gait which marks her breed.

Meanwhile, back at the Reedy barn, the white gander would be waiting. So completely did he identify with the mare that David figures that gander might have taken to saddle and bridle if tack the right size had been handy.

The white long-necked bird grazed faithfully with the white mare, dozed in the sun by her side, walked to the spring in tandem with her for a drink. There was nothing in its life to make it think it wasn't a horse, unless it was our ancient white Ford pickup. Occasionally I'd stop by Mr. Reedy's pasture to watch the mare and the gander graze together, and a couple of times I thought the gander displayed an inordinate interest in becoming a truck.

So the mystery is not that the gander thought it was a horse, but what adventure it saw in crossing over to Ivy Moyers' place to become a cow. Ivy tried to change his mind with a broom, yet this only seemed to intensify the gander's desire to move on to a new experience. He refused to be deterred by the cultural expectation that "such things have never been." He left his equine life behind forever and took up with Mrs. Moyers' mostly-white Holstein. Like a lot of us, the gander had to try out a number of identities before he could settle for who he is today—and he may not be finished yet.

The bird might have suffered a moment of existential doubt the first time he saw Ivy shove a milk-pail under the Holstein. But if his legs were too short for milking, they were long enough for a swim in his—the cow's—water trough.

Consider the gander's freedom; was he restricted in his role by predetermined realism? No, not even to remaining a horse, yet in becoming a cow he did not abandon his historical gooseness; in the presence of water he remembered the utility of his webbed feet. Furthermore, against considerable pressure to conform to common understandings among Mrs. Moyers' leghorn chickens and Guinea fowl, he felt free to be different. His new reality grew on him like—well, like feathers.

* * *

David didn't sue Ivy for alienating the affections of his gander. Community isn't built that way. God builds his kingdom out of compassion and going an extra mile for someone, not out of what we think is right and who is wrong. One of the great burdens of prosperity is our isolation from each other; we don't need neighbors any more, and our lives are diminished. There is serenity in community, in caring for those around us. In discovering what it meant to be neighbors, Norma and I began to find out who we were and why we're here.

* * *

Most of us are flexible about identity. Like Ivy Moyer's goose, we like to think we can try on different guises, maybe see which one we like best or which one fits who we want to be.

Like a chameleon, I tried a few on for size: businessman, outdoor writer, advertising man with a grey flannel heart. By the time we landed in Frog Hollow, I wasn't trying new ones on so much as wondering whether there was anything real under the old disguises.

It became a persistent question: how many of us really know who we are? There are people who know what they want to do early in life, and they are fortunate. But what we do in a career only partly defines who we are.

Like breathing the clean air in the hollow, we gradually inhaled some understanding of integrity from our neighbors. And gradually began to perceive what Jesus was getting at about our real identity and what it took to find it.

The real shape of our becoming is there all right, closer

to us than we imagine. Of a certainty, it is made up in part of family traits, physical limitations, environmental influences, cultural patterns, personal gifts and abilities.

Yet there is more to our identity than the sum of these parts. There has to be more. I believed the new birth the Bible spoke of gave us an opportunity for spiritual growth, whatever that might be. Yet I wasn't prepared for the kind of quantum leap of character and being that the process demanded.

*   *   *

When a member of the ruling council in Judea came to see Jesus privately one night, he brought his pre-packaged ideas of identity with him. What he perceived himself to be isn't made clear in the gospel of John, chapter 3; for all we know, he was a well-adjusted leader in the community and had made his accommodations with the real world around him.

Why he came to Jesus is equally obscure, although Jesus understood the man had questions about his reality. The man started off by praising Jesus for his teaching as a man from God. But Jesus stopped him abruptly, telling the man that if he wanted to know what was real, if he wanted to "see the kingdom of God" as it was, then he'd need to be "born again." Jesus didn't use a term such as mutation or evolution because he didn't know it, yet there is much to indicate that what he had in mind was a mutation/ transformation, a quantum leap from one level of human nature to a new creation, a new identity in a new beginning, to be lived out in power with the same spirit that gave Jesus' life its power.

Jesus pointed out to his visitor that it is an Old Testament idea. Running throughout the Bible is this demand for a transformed character, a metamorphosis of the ordinary brought about by two factors in a symbiotic relationship: the presence of a God more than willing to provide the ability to live on a new and different level, and an open and receptive individual willing to give up all those other half-cooked identities for a consistent, integrated one.

We saw the consistent nature of that identity in some of our neighbors in the hollow, and a new understanding began to take hold. Something about the life we saw in Ivy Moyers and David Reedy and our other neighbors pushed at our ideas of what it means to be a Christian. The impact of their character amounted to more than honesty and integrity and neighborliness. And since it was coupled with the absence of an "aren't I holy" pretentiousness, we found ourselves challenged to consider a new kind of human consciousness lifted to new levels. Truly, a new creation.

FEISTY

6

Seemliness and Reality

The new creature I was called to grow into had to grow away from what I had been up to now and from what I perceived as reality. Circumstances of job and culture are the backdrop to the identities we assume. But God has ways of changing our circumstances, to awaken us to new possibilities, to a new and greater realm. The world I thought I lived in came up against the world of Bill Deavers, our neighbor down along the creek in Frog Hollow. And I discovered God's sense of humor.

People shouldn't visit Bill Deavers in shorts. Not that Bill's prejudiced against Bermudas, like my father was. I never saw my father in shorts, or even in a bathing suit, for that matter. His only concession to the humid summers in Manitoba was to leave off his suit coat. If the heat became excessive, Father would roll up his shirt sleeves and peel off his celluloid collar, but that was as far as he deemed it appropriate to go. I didn't associate Father's style in clothes with his concept of seemliness until after I met Bill Deavers.

Although I've never seen Bill wearing shorts, he'll peel down to his undershirt on a warm Virginia day, and it doesn't have to be too warm a day either. In his 60's, Bill seems mostly leather and meat and energy. It takes a sharp frost to get him to button up the top three buttons on his shirt. Even on a cold spring morning, if he's digging in a fence post or driving some rocks down the hole beside it to firm it up against frost heaving, he'll shuck his shirt if the wind's not blowing. And when I'm taking off my work gloves to blow warm breath on my fingers, he's still working bare-handed.

He's the sort of tough rooster you have to boil all day just to make soup, but as hot as the Valley weather may get, I've never seen him in shorts. I never wondered why until I went to his place one day in my cutoff jeans.

The Deavers place lies along Joe's Creek beside the community cemetery. Bill has a couple of machine sheds, a chicken house, a woodshed, a cattle shelter, a workshop, an outhouse and a few other structures whose purposes change with his job opportunities. He's the best fence builder in the area and takes on miscellaneous bits of construction for the neighbors.

Just recently Bill had fixed up his old house for his new bride. He was proud of his wife, delighted he had someone to talk to, someone to admire and cherish. Hazel's first husband died; they lived on the property next to Bill's and had been his friends for years. I never heard him say it, but I think he was surprised that she consented to marry an old bachelor and take the risks that might involve. But Hazel seemed content. And Bill's life took on a new agenda.

I had borrowed Bill's barbed wire stretchers and wire twister to tighten a piece of fence that Sukey, one of our daughter Cathy's mares, had loosened. It wasn't exactly Sukey's fault. She is a Western bred quarter horse, a flat-lander recently transplanted to our hilly homestead, and maybe from where she was grazing, uphill of the fence, it didn't look much of a barrier.

As can happen with a mare in heat, Sukey became

enamored of Cathy's Arabian stud Taraki in the downhill pasture and thought she might hop on over for a call. She began to run down the hill to join him. Norma and I were having a cup of coffee in the kitchen and Norma pointed out the window.

"I don't think Sukey's going to stop."

At the last moment, the fence must have looked some higher to Sukey than it had before, but since she had already attained a canter, there wasn't much to do but see how good she was at somersaulting. She hit the fence with her chest high enough to add spring to her half-gainer. It wasn't at all graceful, since she landed on her neck and shoulder, but it achieved her purpose and Taraki was happy to oblige.

And that is why the fence needed tightening, and why I was returning Bill's fence tools. Bill told me to put things back where I found them, which took me to his pickup, past a couple of hens and his white rooster. Having visited in their presence fully-dressed a number of times previously, I never gave them a moment's thought.

I heard a noise behind me peculiar enough to turn me around. Bill's white rooster was thundering down the middle of the lane towards my knees, wings out, head thrust forward and blood-lust in his mean, beady eyes. I took an instant hatred to that bird, a feeling that was obviously mutual. I roared at him and made a threatening gesture, realizing a split-second later that my size and arrogance daunted him not a whit. I backed hurriedly to the safety of Bill's pickup and tossed his fence-making tools on the seat where he'd either see them or sit on them, then attended to the matter of survival. My own pickup was at the other end of the lane. That is, on the other side of the rooster who was only momentarily at bay.

This is ridiculous, I thought. I threw a piece of gravel at him and sidled out of the lee of the truck.

"Go on! Get away!" I shouted. But the sight of all that

naked leg inflamed his Puritan wrath, and he bored in. I kicked some gravel in his face. Ah! That slowed him! I began to retreat in haste, kicking gravel while backing, which is possible, but only under extreme circumstances.

Out of the corner of my eye I saw two chickens standing in the bleachers cheering. "Not for me, they're not," I muttered; then, as I receded from them backwards, the victor's crow sounded the end of battle. He had driven the fearsome white-knees from his yard and protected his hens.

When I related the experience to Bill later, he laughed and told me I got off easy. He recalled the time Ray Hollar, who's got a machine shop in town, came to pick up a piece of machinery, and the rooster hit him in the groin before he could defend himself. After Ray got on his feet again, he asked Bill how much he wanted for the bird. Bill said the rooster wasn't for sale. Ray allowed it would be worth ten dollars just to wring its neck.

Hot and all as it gets here, I don't blame Bill for not wearing shorts. When it comes to an anatomical risk of this nature, it just doesn't pay.

*　　*　　*

I suspect a similar anatomical risk was the reason that the Reverend MacDonald let us kids play baseball by ourselves, in the days that followed the Fort Garry United Church of Canada picnic. My experience with Bill's rooster opened the door to both the memory and a flood of new questions to answer.

I don't think I ever knew how Reverend MacDonald came to be the minister of the small country church near the home of my childhood, but thinking back, it was probably a form of retirement. A gentle, white-haired man of much learning, he tried hard to be a part of the community, which is never easy for a stranger, anywhere. He had the benefit of a half-dozen dedicated parishioners to help him feel needed. But there must have been times when the boisterous energy of the neighborhood children made him wish he had chosen another vocation. Or another location.

After the picnic, we started a softball game. Since there weren't enough of us to go around, the Rev — as the children called him — was pressed into service as catcher, for two reasons. One, we were a scrawny bunch and without a backstop we needed some bulk behind the plate to stop the ball. And two, nobody else wanted the job. The perils were obvious; with some of the kids swinging wild, you could get brained with a bat, among other things.

Everything went great until the fourth inning, when Ernie Tippet stepped up to bat. Ernie was the neighborhood's big hitter and took a mean cut at the ball. He hit mostly home runs, because there was nobody who could throw the ball even halfway home from as far as he could hit it. So he'd trot around the bases, laughing as small fry like me out in the hayfield tried to find the ball and run back to find somebody we could heave it to.

Everybody got a little nervous when Ernie stepped to the plate, hoping he wouldn't hit it their way. I used to grieve at spending all my time out in far left field, several layers removed from the action. But with Ernie up to bat, I hoped fervently the action would happen somewhere else, and I think most of the half dozen little kids in the outfield felt the same way. One thing nobody wanted to be right then was the pitcher.

Alice Queens was a pretty good pitcher, with a squirrely windup that usually made me swing before the ball was anywhere near the plate. But Ernie didn't care what she did with the ball or how weird her windup looked. He'd hit a low fast one or a high slow pitch just as easily, never missing a beat in the rhythm of chewing his gum. We weren't allowed to chew gum in Sunday School, and some kids thought he tipped the ball back at Reverend MacDonald to get even for the times he'd been asked to spit out his wad. But I never thought it was anything but an accident, although Ernie was happy to accept the notoriety.

Alice wound up and let fly with a fast one, low and on the inside, where Ernie would miss if he was going to. But he got a piece of it, and the ball snapped back into the dirt in a wicked bounce that caught Reverend MacDonald crouched over and in an exposed position. There's no time to react in a situation like that; you either get hit somewhere or you don't. League ballplayers wear chest-pads and other accoutrements for protection, but in a scratch game, nobody comes equipped.

Humility is a great asset, and it often starts as humiliation. Reverend MacDonald survived his ordeal with humble dignity, more or less. Some of his parishioners acknowledged that it wasn't what could be called dignified to writhe around in the dust at home plate, but these observers were all men and understood the situation. They weren't all that dignified themselves, since most found the situation conducive to mirth and several chose to walk away quickly rather than join the boys—and the Reverend—in rolling on the ground, trying to breathe again.

Alice Queens had more sense than the rest of us. Although she walked off the mound with a kind of wild grinny look in her eye, she kept her dignity and in some ways restored Reverend MacDonald's too. To see the Rev suffering on the ground at home plate drew compassion from all the men and boys. Yet I have wondered since if some of the laughter, repressed as it was, came because of his role as guardian of our souls. My father did not laugh; it wasn't seemly. He may have smirked a little, but he would not laugh. Furthermore, he did not see the Reverend MacDonald as guardian of *his* soul.

* * *

My father did not attend church services any more often than he could help, since he did not admire Reverend MacDonald's approach. He considered the man's preaching an intellectual morass into which the innocent and unwary could fall and lose their way. His antipathy toward the elderly clergyman was not helped by the telephone.

My father and elder brothers had begun a small business, the business that would eventually become Fairfield & Sons, behind our house, and the telephone soon became an essential instrument. Back in the early 1930s, everyone who could afford a telephone got one. Ours was a big wall-mounted device with a separate earpiece and a mouthpiece arching out of the front of the oak cabinet like the neck of a goose. You cranked a handle on the side of the instrument to summon the operator, who could listen to your conversation if she wished to—and often did.

A number of homes were on our multi-party line, but no one used it more than my father, unless it was Reverend MacDonald. The church and manse were only three vacant lots removed from our place. The two men spent a lot of time on the telephone, Father speaking to suppliers and buyers, Reverend MacDonald hearing the problems of a parishioner or arranging church functions with his elders. No matter the reason, Father believed the minister should do his telephone calling in the evening and leave the line free during the day for the needs of honest working people.

It got so that Father would come into the house from the mill and crank the ringer to initiate a call before listening first, as was considered polite, to find out if anyone was already on the line. If he discovered he was interrupting one of our other neighbors' use of the line, he would hang up and wait a reasonable length of time before trying again. If it was Reverend MacDonald, however, Father would smile grimly and demand, "I need the line."

Trying to arrange a meeting one day with several

businessmen in Winnipeg, my father competed with Reverend MacDonald all morning for the use of the telephone. Each time he found the minister on the line, Father brusquely demanded he get off. As his frustration grew, his language became more colorful. Mother tried to shush him, but I don't think he heard her, so focused was his attention.

He picked up the receiver again, then crashed it down. "Old fool," he raged. Frightened, I picked up the board I had been hammering on and grabbed for mother's hand. We could hear him counting to himself, "Eight, nine, TEN."

He picked up the receiver again, listened a moment, then shouted, "Get off the damned line!" Mother hustled me out through the front door and handed me the hammer.

My sister Margaret always knew when I was upset and pounced on my fears as a way to develop new male-management skills. As a seven-year-old, I didn't understand or appreciate her fourteen-year-old need to sharpen such techniques.

I don't recall exactly how Margie did it that day. It was nothing as crude as, "You were a mistake and Mother should send you back." She was much more subtle, using, perhaps, "Jenny Bowles loves you."

Now that hurt. It didn't even need to be true. The *possibility* was enough to make a seven-year-old strike back.

Margie hurled her accusation as she came out the front door onto the porch where I was hammering another nail into the board. She took off so fast I didn't have time to put down the hammer before I gave chase.

With longer legs and greater speed, she rounded the house ahead of me and escaped through the kitchen door. But I could see her through the window. The good news? My aim was off. The bad news? I broke the window. I missed my sister, but I hit my father square between the shoulder blades.

Perhaps the hammer blow was retribution for my father's

telephone behavior, if one believes justice is always so swift. Unfortunately, the sword of justice cuts both ways. Father whirled to see who was responsible; then I could see him drop the telephone receiver and head for the back door.

Humiliation is often well-deserved. With instincts in full control, I believed that a man like my father could run faster than a small boy like me, unless I started before he did. I didn't start soon enough. He caught me before I got to sanctuary at the church, three lots down the road, where he reinforced my decision not to throw a hammer at anybody again, least of all him. It wasn't seemly.

*　　*　　*

That's about as close as my father wanted to get to the church. Mother exerted a certain pious influence, coupled with the religious calendar, so that he might take up Easter or Thanksgiving as a time to refresh his acquaintance with the little stone building and its standardized faith. Summers were busy, and Father didn't see value in winter attendance; he complained the building needed more warmth than it achieved from the stove that greeted worshipers as they walked in the door. But he used to say that at least it was a warmer greeting than he ever got from old Quinter, the chief usher. Quinter was in fact the only usher, since not that many attended regularly. For special events like Thanksgiving, Quinter would press a few of the local men into service to help seat people and lift the offering.

It was my father's contention that this was the principal function of the church, to lift offerings, or, rephrasing one of the philosophers he read, "to lift the burden of money from the poor." He said the other, less obvious function was to replace the burden of money with a heavier burden of guilt. Never one to mince words, he told Mother as we left church after one particularly evangelical Thanksgiving sermon, "If that old vulture calls me a sinner like that one more time, I'll kick his backside into next week."

Mother shushed him and covered her embarrassment with a bright comment on the weather to the preacher's wife, and did she think we would get snow this week? It was a safe diversion. We could always get snow in Manitoba, and people were challenged to ever more creative complaints about the fierce demands of natural events—flood and humidity, heat and mosquitoes, winter's wind chill and when the ice might break up on the river to bring the floods again.

My father resented the easy answers of popular evangelists. The only cleric who held his interest for any length of time was Harry Emerson Fosdick in his radio sermons from New York. Not that Father had better answers for his life than the evangelists; he spent much of his mature years trying to understand reality in a time of terrifying change. A virtual orphan, my father had been sent out from England before the turn of the century in one of those waves of unwanted children who were shipped to the colonies to live with whoever would take them, in his case a middle-aged aunt who moved on to California two years later, leaving my father with an accommodating family of Scots.

These cultural orphans had been abandoned by family, by the people of the community—relatives, friends, teachers, shopkeepers—and even by the church, the one institution which claimed best to represent love, mercy and justice. The experience stamped its mark indelibly on my father, and everyone who lived with him sensed his struggle to be accepted.

He read widely in an attempt to understand and mitigate the empty spaces in his life. Jesus told the crowd, "Blessed are those who hunger and thirst for righteousness, for they shall be filled." My father longed for something credible in his life. He found little comfort in religion and philosophy, yet he could not leave them alone. Despite the chaos of his life—or perhaps because of it—my father looked for and found order. Seemliness. While this may not have smoothed the roughness of his speech, orderliness in custom became his style. It may even have become his religion, although he would have denied it, of course.

Ivy Moyers would say that my father tried too hard. In one way or another, most of us try too hard when we build our realities, trying to keep God under control in a life-tight compartment. As a strategy for living, it may seem to work at times, but we should never count on it—we might miss the real thing. And miss out on what we are called to become.

* * *

The significance of Jesus, as we were beginning to discover in Frog Hollow, is not that he worked miracles or began a new religion. Rather, he saw a greater reality and tried to describe it to whoever would listen. He told stories beginning with "the kingdom of God is like...," and each parable projected a facet of his insight. The kingdom he saw clashed with the world he moved in, a world not unlike our own now, where power and prestige and privilege made the rules for everyone else to live by. Jesus rejected that reality and described a greater one where the poor counted, and where enemies forgave enemies. Think what that could mean in Ireland and the Middle East, for starters.

If he couldn't bring people to live in that reality any other way, it was Something Jesus knew was worth dying for.

WILDLIFE

7

Learning from the Land

Like my father, Bill Deavers believed in Something that ordered the universe, however undisciplined the universe may seem. Nature is always an adventure, always coloring predictable science with extravagant art. Plant X acres of corn to get Y bushels of feed—if enough chemical fertilizer is applied: that's the science. The art? God may not seem real to some chemists, but out here in the hollow, nature produces its evidence in every blade of grass. Watch a half dozen yearling deer chase each other around a pasture, hear a veery echo its cathedral song in the woods, smell the sweet of locust blossoms on a spring morning—the Creator-Sustainer is here, conducting the orchestra.

We haven't applied ourselves enough to the arts of nature, to understanding its whims and gallantries. Some Amish farmers plant by the phases of the moon, but drought comes to their land just as it does to their neighbors'. El Nino hurries showers to some areas, floods to others, and we don't know how much our actions are involved. If technology has brought us to new levels of food production, it has also shown us how little we know about the effects of human activity on the environment. And make no mistake, a healthy environment is necessary for our future.

Our neighbors in the hollow are as confused about the environment as the rest of the country is. But they've taught us this much: *we're in this world together.* We're all part of the food chain, and what we do on our land inevitably involves others, animal, vegetable and mineral. Horticultural sprays drift downwind. Horses need to be fenced out as much as fenced in. "Blessed are the merciful, for they will receive mercy," comes across like "Care for your neighbor as you would have him care for you."

I was building another fence one Saturday. Wrestling barbed wire will never replace fishing as a hobby, but Cathy's horses had taken to browsing deeper in the woods. After a two-year drought, we were a little short on pasture and long on stock, so in early spring I had turned some animals in to what we had hoped would become wilderness.

Now, we didn't mind too much the wineberry canes getting trimmed back; they were getting out of hand anyway. It did hurt us to see the young trees being pruned so short—but as hard as the animals were on the trees, the real bite was on the wildflowers. Norma has identified many varieties in those woods. Hepatica. Bloodroot. Rue-anemone. False Solomon's-seal. Mayapple. Jack-in-the-pulpit.

I had told her the stock wouldn't bother with the deep woods itself. Several weeks after they'd been turned in, Norma took me looking for Mayapples where she knew there was a clump in the deep woods. We couldn't find a single stalk where hundreds had grown the year before.

She didn't say anything close to "I told you so," though well she might have, such was the measure of the loss she felt. Instead she made light of her dismay and pointed out how the animals' paths made it so much easier to walk through the underbrush.

What good are wildflowers anyway? How vital are

they in the grand scheme? There are so many terribly important things in life—the next stock market crash, world overpopulation, corruption in government and business, the simmering energy crisis—of what possible value can a few wildflowers be to anyone?

There aren't answers to questions like that. For most of us, jobs count ahead of the environment. For many, energy is more important than landscape. For some, so is the freedom to throw pop bottles and beer cans out of the car window.

And wildflowers? Utilitarian values they have not. They do nothing to entertain us except grow. We have to hunt them out, and there's not much to them when they're found. So plow them under, pave them over—or turn in the livestock and let the wildflowers at least provide fodder, build hamburger, produce milk.

Norma says a lot by not saying anything. Sometimes. So in spite of all the other necessary chores, protecting the wildflowers became a priority. I picked up some barbed wire at the co-op and set out to fence the horses into a four-acre patch along the lower creek.

Which is how I came to be within earshot of our neighbor Alec Bristol; I'd heard he had an angry mouth and now I believe it. He took offense at another Frog Hollow resident, Ferlin Johnson, and let him know how annoyed he had become. When Alec is annoyed, his verbal repertoire can blister paint.

Alec's place is just below ours, a small plot of land on Joe's Creek where he lives alone on his Social Security. Alec seems to get along by himself; with no one else to tell him how to eat, he likes to fry up a slice or two of baloney and heat some onion rings or fries in the oven. Slathered with chili sauce, it'd kill most any stomach but his, so he "neutralizes" the acid/fat potential with a dish of ice cream; about any shade will do. The only time he ever really got in dietary difficulty was when a couple of Jehovah's Witnesses came by between courses and Alec figured to make them nervous by offering a companionable chew of Red Man, which he forgot to remove before returning to his bowl of Strawberry Delight.

The day in consideration, two strands of wire were up and I was running a third down the hill behind our place when Alec fired his first salvo. Seems he laid claim to a piece of land Ferlin Johnson says is his. Alec put up a board fence around it, a kind of "whatsoever ye put your foot on to possess" sort of thing.

So Ferlin put his foot down too. One day he decided he didn't want a fence on his property, so he dismantled Alec's efforts.

To suggest the obvious, no one likes to build any more fence than he has to, and Alec took some displeasure at the loss of his efforts. This particular morning he was reminding Ferlin and anyone else within earshot how little he appreciated the situation.

Whether Ferlin responded I was not able to discern. There weren't any responseful pauses in the discourse, but then again, such was the nature of the oration that a pause would have been inharmonious.

It seems Ferlin Johnson has deed to the small strip of land in debate. It is also audibly noticeable that Alec perceives the property to be his through tenure. And while Ferlin may have additional reasons for pressing his claim, I suspect he finds some masochistic adventure in provoking Alec.

Some of us like wildflowers. Some like to spit in the wind.

*   *   *

We're pushed up against choices continually. Bill Deavers didn't want us to let our hillside go back to wilderness. We should be using it, he told us, grazing it, cutting it, doing something with it.

"But letting it go *is* doing something with it," I muttered back at him.

Bill had come round to help me set up the Gravely garden tractor I'd bought at an auction in the village. I was pulling some honeysuckle off a gate post when he drove up in his truck—honeysuckle will cover the world one day, if kudzu doesn't get there first. When Bill took it upon himself to point out the error of our ways, I tried to explain. After all, why *shouldn't* we let nature take over?

"We want to let the wild animals have a place to live," I tried again. Bill is a gentleman of the mountain sort, and after a deprecatory snort, he changed the subject, leaving me to think of all my good arguments later. He didn't want to spoil the morning with an argument.

I couldn't get Bill's comments out of my mind. Norma and I felt good about letting the hill go back to wilderness. We planted some evergreen seedlings here and there in the open spots on the hill to encourage the process. But maybe we were wrong. In a world where hunger is a terrible truth, is the concept of "wilderness" an offense against humanity?

What can anyone do for land as used up as this? I wondered that evening as I walked up the hill behind our house. Only part of our 34 acres was pasture; the 20-acre hillside was its dominant feature. Oldtimers in Frog Hollow say this hillside once yielded corn to the plow. Little wonder its topsoil had slid off into the washes and flats.

I looked down at the ground and saw its open wounds. Canker sores of clay stared up between threadbare patches of orchard grass and moss and limestone outcrops. It wouldn't have produced much corn before it became a pasture for cattle, and poor pasture at that. Rising from the tiny spring branch at its feet, the hill that lay before me should never have known any hoof but that of the Virginia deer.

When we bought the place, the land had lain fallow for a number of years. The hillside had begun to sprout its woody weeds—wild rose, persimmon, locust, juniper, sumac, scrub pine, and "tree of heaven." (The man who gave the ailanthus its common name probably swore like that at his livestock too.)

When we first moved in, Bill Deavers advised us, "Cut out all that trash and turn in some beef." Bill can talk like that because his place on the other side of the hill looks pastorally pleasant and well managed. He has skillfully teetered along the thin edge between overworked land and survival. But Bill has been willing to work for his farm as well as live off it.

Bill Deaver's balancing act on his farm is different from so many of the small farmers of the Shenandoah Valley. As many small holdings become unprofitable and farmers begin to work in town at the muffler plant or the feed mills, their farms become a moonlighting occupation. While some smallholders do a reasonable job of moonlighting, many— like me—haven't the energy left at day's end to match their dreams. So the fences fray, the manure doesn't get spread to fertilize the fields, a severe rain starts a gully on the hill, and the slow process of degeneration begins.

So maybe leaving the land to heal itself is the least we can do for our place. And the best. Because now that we've fenced our horses and sheep out of the woods, the hill is on its way back to native trees and flowers. Ground-hugging dewberries provide a binder against further erosion. Clumps of wineberries and mountain blackberries give us a magnificent crop for the freezer and jam jar and provide protection for the young tree sprouts that are coming along. Fulfilling a similar function is a scattering of junipers and scrub pine, serving as cover trees in the young woods.

Along the old cornfield on the hill where all this activity is taking place is our woodlot, with its variety of oaks to prove its advanced state. As the Virginia commonwealth forester whom we asked for advice pointed out, oaks are the evidence of a terminal forest, the final evolution from blackberry canes and softwood growth. He wanted us to improve the stand by clearing out all of the redbuds and dogwoods and wild roses which scatter along the edges.

But the state conservation agents who encouraged our wilderness experiment pointed out that these trees provide food and cover for a host of birds and small animals. Except in the state forests, the number of acres providing natural cover for local wildlife dwindles every year.

What advantage can a small wilderness area bring to our world? I don't know, but if the beauty and dignity of a natural stand of trees isn't enough, there's the argument for the preservation of natural woods. Not just orderly rows of cultured loblolly pines like the forester wanted us to plant. Pine plantations are great for timber, and the loblolly is a fine tree, but...

Instead, the wild profusion of native trees makes the hill a fascination of color and shape—sycamore, cherry, persimmon (Norma makes a nice dessert bread out of the ripe fruit we share with the raccoons and deer), hickory, locust, sassafras, and many kinds of oak.

And wildlife is returning. This summer we watched deer—two does and four fawns—browse their way through the brush. Quail and pileated woodpeckers allow themselves to be seen occasionally. Foxes, raccoons and possum are in the deep brush beyond the hillcrest. And the day we see a bear, we'll have fulfilled the promise of a hiding place for wildlife. It will scare the pucky out of us and probably mean fewer and more cautious berry pickings, but it will be another proof of nature's potential for recovery.

Maybe there is more that should be done for our hillside, but at least giving it a chance to heal itself is a start. It takes little or no effort on our part, just as long as we stop adding to the problem.

So when I found the patch of raw soil where cover should have been, I looked up the hill at those scruffy weed trees the foresters wanted us to bulldoze or spray with herbicides. Those weed trees are the hope of the hill, binding into place what remains of the plowed-over topsoil.

Between the trunks of the locusts, the new canes of wild blackberries form another clump of hope, each succeeding crop adding a shadow-thin layer of humus: rotting canes, trapped leaves, bird droppings, building back in God's time a soil we have drained away in ours.

* * *

There are so many illusions laying claim to shaping us now, including the idea that we know what is best for the environment, or that we aren't really hurting nature by what we're doing, or that free enterprise will always do what is right for the future. Everything in our world tends to push God to one side; we are in charge here and what we do with the world is our concern. But all such illusions need to be pounded out on the anvil of reality—and it has to do with much more than the land and water and air we take for granted.

Our experiences in Frog Hollow began to show us that it wasn't that our reality included God but that God was the reality that included us. It's not a perception to come by easily; furthermore, in Frog Hollow we learned that while God would recreate us in a new way of living, he would never force that change of perspective upon us. Maybe that's the risk in faith we were eager to avoid, that God might lead us in a way we would not choose. Look what happened to Jesus. So leave me my choices, Lord.

But as we were to discover, that's precisely the point: God leaves the choices to us, always has and always will, even the choice to follow his leading. So maybe the good news is that God has elegant ways of helping us survive all our choices, good or bad. That is, of course, if we'll let him—a process I continue to find elusive, and will to the end of my days, I suspect. But that complicates what is really much simpler: God loves us.

Even the land expresses the forgiveness of God. We scrape it bare, yet in a few years of freedom it offers back to us wild blackberries as evidence of grace.

MOUNTAIN FAITH

8

Mountain Faith

Exploring what seems most important to me right now comes under the category of exploring our culture and its religion, although people in the hollow don't talk about them much. Opinions on culture can be as obscure as differences in religion, and talking might stir up doctrinal prejudices and cultural pretensions better held in check.

Norma and I have enjoyed our share of pretensions, and I don't know whether we learned much from the experience or just got tired of trying to rewrite our personal history. One thing we did learn was that it's all right for people to be different. In fact, maybe that's the most useful form of forgiving others their trespasses—forgiving differences. If we can learn to forgive people for being different from our expectations of them, it'll be a cinch to stop abusing them for disagreeing with our religion. Or our politics.

Our neighbor Ivy Moyers has a very simple religion—no, that's not quite right—she has a simple and well-exercised *faith*. For Ivy, God is God, and knows exactly what he's doing. While he is working out whatever it is he has in mind for the nations, he still has enough grace and more to pity the sparrows and all the other little people of the world. She knows, because over the long hard years of her life God has loved her, and worked some blessings into her days. When her husband died and she still had two children at home to care for, she scratched a living for them from her patch of land. And God was there to help her.

No, he didn't pick up an axe and chop her kindling. Her boys were big enough; even the oldest, who were already married, found time to chop and pile her firewood.

Well, that's her boys helping her out, not God. "True," she'd say, "but they feel good about helping me." That's just psychological feedback for altruism. "Maybe. I don't understand that kind of thing. But I know God loves us and helps us love others; why shouldn't we feel good? Call it anything you like, that won't change it."

Ivy isn't overpowered by heavyweight argument; she knows she has a limited education, but that doesn't mean she must deny her native wisdom. Or her experiences of faith. She knows that children don't have to love their parents or do things for them. There are lots of kids in the world around her who don't give a damn about their kinfolk. Her children could treat her like that, too, but they don't, and that's what God has done for her, thank you.

*   *   *

Jesus said something like, "Blessed are the pure-hearted, the people with integrity, for they will see God." That is what God will look like, Integrity itself, and like Ivy, those with integrity will recognize him; essence will respond to Essence. Jesus painted another picture; in working out who we are becoming, we'll be paired with Essence itself. Like one of a team of oxen plowing new ground in the reality of God, we'll be yoked with the same spirit Jesus knew.

Ivy understood this agricultural picture and, yoked with

Jesus, she worked out her own pure-heartedness. Her faith put together a profound theological insight without having to spell it out in words. Sometimes religion can become oversold on explanations; a certain amount of intelligent input doesn't hurt, but it isn't the necessary ingredient.

*   *   *

The wide-ranging faith we saw in the hollow began to stir some ideas. I began to see faith involving us in much more than being reconciled to the Unknown God through Jesus, his human expression and evidence. I began to see that faith is our means of becoming part of the greater reality that God is still creating, what Jesus called the "kingdom of God."

Humans have been evolving into something more than we were when we started out ever since we had the spirit of life breathed into us. Back in the mists of time we had learned to walk; now we can fly. We had learned to talk; now we can communicate across oceans. But these are simple physical developments compared to the demands of Greater Reality. How do we achieve integrity, honor, kindliness, humility—and achieve them consistently? What evolutionary leap will it take for us to overcome hatred and learn to love those who would be our enemies?

Jesus was far from naive when he lifted up forgiveness, love and righteousness as the marks of the "new birth" he described. In effect, he demonstrated the new humanity living in a new community, and spent the few years he had explaining what this Greater Reality looked like. In response, a growing number of people began to live with a growing understanding of an expanded and expanding existence. Their lives changed in profound ways, a mutation in who they were and what they were becoming.

With such a host of believers pointing the way, we have a better understanding of faith and its role in connecting us to the grace of a still-creating God, creating a new humanity in a new community of grace.

* * *

Back when Ivy Moyers was a teenager—since there wasn't a bowling alley or a movie house or a tavern anywhere close in living memory—going to church turned out to be the most exciting event of the week. She and her family walked six miles down off the mountain where her folks had their homestead. Neighbors joined up with them along the way, and the walk to and from church became an eight hour visit interrupted by a couple of hours of preaching and praying and singing. You could catch up on all the news of the area, find out who had a deer eating up her garden or why one churchgoer, Ethel Rose, had a bandage on her left hand all the way to her elbow (the handle on her wash tub broke when she lifted it off the cookstove; good thing her wash had stopped boiling, or the scald would have gone too deep).

Ivy's friend Alcie May, who was four years older than Ivy, hung back until Wayne Wilfong caught up. After the other Wilfong kids stopped teasing Wayne and went back to playing tag and kicking stones, Wayne held Alcie May's hand. Alcie's nine-year-old brother R. J. had an inner-tube rubber slingshot for shooting squirrels, at which he was rarely successful. On the way to church, he traded the use of that slingshot to his buddy Frank Whissen for a ride on his two-wheeler. Frank didn't mind trading since they were down off the mountain and climbing a long grade over the ridge before the Evangelical United Brethren Church at Locust Grove, but when he wanted his bicycle back at the top of the ridge, R.J. said he'd see him at the church and sailed on down the slope past a line of girls he hoped would admire his fearless form.

That particular Sunday was the start of revival week, and the preacher from away had already started calling on the homes on the mountain, steered around to the most appropriate places by the pastor, Edward Boyer. "Most appropriate" on the first day of visiting depended on who Pastor Boyer thought might welcome them; he did not want to cast the visiting pearl before too many swine until the evangelist got his bearings. "Appropriate" also led them to Alcie May's house just before her mother hammered on the dinner gong, a triangle of wrought iron hanging from a leather thong outside the back door.

Back then most folks on the mountain received their preachers with penitential hospitality, and Doris Seybolt, Alcie May's mother, could make her humble offerings of green beans and fatback taste like a bishop's fare. And the pie she made from wild blackberries was "sinful good" according to the evangelist. Pastor Boyer smiled and took the compliment to his good judgment and timing.

The EUB churches were more progressive than the River Baptists or the Mennonites. Back when Ivy was a girl, the Evangelical United Brethren were still strict about dancing, smoking, and drinking—as were the other mountain churches—but somehow there was a difference that made the EUB's too worldly for serious believers.

Maybe this ill-defined difference was the reason the EUB evangelist was so warmly received, even in the homes of the sinners or those others who had fallen by the wayside and were fair game for visitation. Nor had Pastor Boyer alienated his neighbors by preaching fire and brimstone. He would not judge sinners, he told his flock; judgment was God's business, not his. He had been called only to love the sinner, not send him to hell.

Jesus would have approved. As he pointed out, "salvation" is really a process in our grace-development rather than a lone transition point, and if we try to second guess where someone else is in the pipeline, we're apt to make judgments about them that only God can make. Instead, we need to make judgments about ourselves if we're going to grow into the image of God.

*   *   *

Ivy Moyers had the wisdom to recognize evil when she saw it and avoid it like the plague. But like the rest of us, she had her struggles with the grey areas, the tough choices, the ambiguities. It was her patience with the ambiguities that gave Norma and me an idea of how to wend our way through our own grey areas by trust in the grace-full leading of God. It is never easy to hear and know the leading of God, especially when we're impatient to get through the maze to where we aim to go. So it's hard to let ourselves be recreated willingly into something new when we haven't gotten there yet.

Ivy didn't have the kind of choices her great-grandchildren face. Life today is different, overwhelmed by the metropolitan flavor we pick up in the very air we breathe.

Nobody will argue with Ivy about the amount of change she has seen in her lifetime. Yet in spite of the mysteries of the Internet, technological developments are still easier to understand than human nature and the changes it has swallowed. In Ivy's lifetime, women have won new freedoms, yet still stumble over their opportunities. And men are more confused than ever.

When we get too far off the track, psychology, psychiatry and their kin can help us adapt to our insecurities. Yet none of the soft sciences have more than scratched the surface of human nature. Men don't really understand themselves, let alone women—although it's fun trying. And frustrating.

So if it's so difficult to get in touch with who we are inside, male or female, how much more difficult is it to understand the workings of God and his nature? Like getting to know a spouse, it takes years of patient surrender of our own ideas to let new awareness break through. And the best chance we have to see the future of "the kingdom of God" is to see his nature at work in people of faith. Yet we see through a glass darkly, with lots of smudges and fingerprints and false impressions on the visible surface.

* * *

Ivy's world has changed, as it has changed for all of us. Even the religion she grew up with is not quite the same. When Ivy was young, the mountain churches were simple buildings, like the simple homes of the members. Today's churches are far more elaborate and expensive. People are better off financially; even their religion is wealthier and more comfortable now, not like the matter of naked trust it used to be for folks who struggled on the edge of survival. Such an insulated religion is a sidebar to the real thrust of an emerging new humanity, the "body of Christ" as the New Testament pictured it.

Jesus said the poor were close to the kingdom of God, because their lives were a matter of trust, in God and in each other. During the Depression of the thirties, survival in the mountains depended on good (or reasonably good) health. If you could stay healthy, there were occasional odd jobs to trade for cash or kind, there was a garden to plant, and there was game in the woods to hunt for the table. But just as it is now for most of the people in the rest of the world, if you tore a muscle, had an appendix go sour or a bad tooth poison your system, or dropped a log on your foot, all you had was God and the caring love of his people.

The community of caring people was the living evidence of the God that Ivy and her neighbors believed in. His reality gave them courage and a goal. Work hard at what God is calling you to be, do right by your neighbor, and God could be trusted to look after the rest.

*   *   *

But work at what? How do we figure out what God is calling us to be? What we do is a large part of what we are, and finding out what we are to do with our days can be confusing and frustrating.

Our friend John Schaefer figures his kids have more choices in what to do with their lives than they—and their emerging faith—know how to handle. One day I caught John clearing out around the culvert under the road in front of his place, and after the usual pleasantries I asked him if his kids were going to follow him on the dairy farm like he had followed his father.

John leaned his shovel against the fence. "No, don't think so, Jim. Looks like Andrew might do something in construction when he gets out of school, and Paula says she wants to be a nurse, maybe as a missionary, would you believe?"

"Not that they don't like the farm. Paula'd like to keep the place always, she says. But they see me banging my head on a post; it's too hard to make a living anymore. So unless something changes, I'll probably sell my herd when I get tired of being stupid."

John leaned on the fence by his shovel; he was easy to distract from his chores if you got to talking farming. Or questioned him about what makes children build a life different from their parents.

"It wouldn't bother me if both our kids stayed with us after they finished high school." John kicked a stone and blew his nose with his thumb. I moved his shovel out of the way and took up a fresh lean on his fence.

"I've seen too many who want to get away from parents so they're free, they figure," he continued. "But I tell our kids independence never comes free."

"Me and Elaine have been letting Andrew loose. He's got that old '66 Mustang to spend his time on, and his girl's smart enough for both of them. If they want to get married and live with us till they land on their feet, that's fine. He might be easier to live with then."

What would tell Andrew he'd landed right? Wasn't John grooved to be a farmer because his father had been one and both hadn't known any better?

John hitched up his jeans. "Don't get smart, Jim, you haven't got the head for it." He slapped dust off his knee, and a crow sifting by overhead dove sideways at the noise. "Today, kids've got a lot more choices beside the farm, and that's better than it used to be. They learn about them at school, but most don't learn what else it takes to make a choice till they're out doing something awhile."

"How's Andrew know what he can do in construction until he does a little? Paula knows a girl, her father spent a fortune going to medical school, then gave it up. Now he's in real estate and happy as my dog."

I asked what that had to do with farming or the price of overalls.

"You asked how Andrew would figure what he wants to do. The kids say the counselor at school's no more good than legs on an egg. Some business people been there to give a talk about jobs, and they got booklets about different occupations, but how does a kid know he wants to do something until he works at it a while?"

"I don't feel guilty for not knowing what to tell Andrew any more'n I feel guilty for being a farmer."

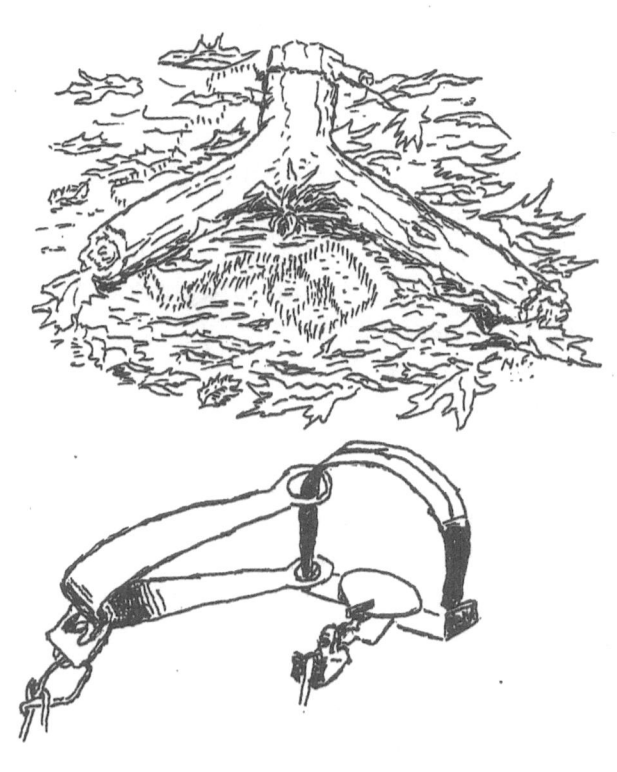

FOOTHOLD TRAP

9

A Matter of Guilt

When it comes to choosing what we do in life, John Schaefer thinks some of us are pushed around by our sense of guilt. "So we're not really free," he says, "to 'do justice, love mercy and walk humbly with our God.' For a lot of people, religion *is* guilt; if you don't feel guilt, your religion isn't doing you any good. After all, guilt's what separates humans from animals, right?"

I suggested he ought to feel ashamed, then, for leaning on the fence when he should be working, but he hardly took a breath. He had another bit in his teeth.

"Guilt's weird, Jim. Some people ought to feel ashamed—a man who hurts somebody else deliberately ought to feel guilt so he'll change and maybe make things right. Like I don't know how these crack dealers sleep easy after selling some kids the drugs that'll kill 'em sooner or later."

John plowed on, saying how most of us like to feel shame; it helps develop a reasonable sense of our own value.

"Guilt's important to the North American economy." John stopped as if he'd been caught talking too much. He looked at me sheepishly and picked up his shovel. "Hey, I got to get back to work—my bank makes me feel ashamed for owing them money. Come by again and we'll talk some more."

I climbed into the pickup, but John had one more thought.

"Seems we *need* guilt," he said, leaning into the cab. "Some say love makes the world go round—nice try but no prize. Bankers believe cash can move mountains, but what we'll do for guilt we'd *never* do for love or money. And if we enjoy it enough, then we'll share it around; what's the good of feeling guilty if you can't make others feel bad, too?"

So much for evangelism, I thought, as I left John digging out his culvert once more.

* * *

Back when I went to Sunday School, Reverend MacDonald wasn't able to get through to the kids in his parish. Most of the girls thought he was a nice old man, maybe a little drifty but kind and well-meaning. The boys didn't waste time thinking about the qualities of grown men like fathers or preachers, except to discover how and if they could be manipulated. The Rev had forgotten that particular phase of his development, so he believed he might influence us as we grew in size, hoping to impart the wisdom we needed to go with it.

The girls, it seems to me, accepted most adults for what they were and took at least some of their advice to heart; they became knowledgeable women long before their hormones got them into trouble. And women at that age seem to have an innate understanding of the foibles of humankind, so they're wary of sin—or at least aware of it—and tend to know what to do about guilt.

But the boys figured official sin was a shuck, and as a consequence didn't know how to handle it. That's why we needed guilt, and why the Rev wanted the boys in his church to feel the weight of shame whether they fully understood the wages of sin or not. Sort of "Guilt is a matter of broken law; Shame is a matter of guilty conscience." He had an uphill struggle and wasn't too successful.

For some of the older boys in our Sunday School class, to drill a hole in the girls outhouse or, even better, to push the outhouse over with them in it, ranked as a sturdy level of achievement and was regarded as sport, not transgression. For the rest of us younger savages, we sought a little elasticity in cussing, stealing marbles or fighting at recess—also recognized as sporting activities.

As occasion demanded, the Rev thundered against sin as a convinced Covenanter in the style of his Scots-Presbyterian training. He told us the Bible said all mankind was as filthy rags, menstrual rags at that, which at our age was a confusing metaphor at best and not at all convincing. Or, he informed us, like sheep we had gone astray, but since few farmers in our part of Manitoba risked keeping sheep because of the long and brutal winters, this image didn't connect either.

If the Rev had been as succinct as my father, he might have thought of a word picture to clarify in our minds what a sinner looked like in the eyes of God, but since most of us called each other similar things anyway, it would not have created a demand for change. It was one thing to be called a butthead; it was another to take it seriously and worry about it.

Mr. Pettis, the Sunday School superintendent, took a more modern approach. He made us aware of the Bible stories so that, like it or not, we began to identify with the good guys and the bad guys, the heroes and the villains. We began to see ourselves against the universal scope of righteousness. We therefore became sinners. For me, as for most of the boys in the "Intermittent" Class at Sunday School, the knowledge didn't make sin any less attractive, but dangerously more so. We might stir up the wrath of God.

The result of the Rev's preachments and Mr. Pettis's stories was a stirring of guilt, a nebulous cloud of unworthiness gathering on our lives to hamper the turbulent boisterousness. Guilt is a powerful device in the hands of the transmitters of culture. It was not good to lie or cheat or steal—or eat with your mouth open, pick your nose, break wind in class, slouch, forget to close your fly, or interrupt your elders. One seemed to be as unworthy as the other, and imposed a strain on new guilt muscles. Thank you, God, that most of the time my own particular elders were busy, and my dog didn't offer judgment.

* * *

Guilt may push on the conscience, but it doesn't do much to point to the reality of God. Jesus spent most of his energies trying to make clear there was something far more important than rules to live by. How we treat others, how we *serve* others, makes our new role in the reality of God much simpler to understand. It's a matter of learning how God's integrity works, how his power to love can reach through our lives to others in order to become neighbor and friend.

I learned this far too late for Morris.

My best friend Morris turned seven just before I did that winter. He didn't go to Sunday School. None of the half-Cree, half-Scottish kids did, at least none that I remember, and I used to wonder why. Like his brothers, Morris wasn't about to be educated in the ways of guilt and wouldn't understand what all the fuss was about.

The part-Cree kids didn't worry too much about anything, it seemed to me. They were much better at catching a ball than I was, and knew how to fish for pickerel and bass and big channel cats in the river. Morris and his family lived in the woodlot next to the golf course at Lower Fort Garry, and his older brothers made good money finding golf balls in the bush along the fifth hole. Any balls that Morris and I found we had to turn over to his brothers; they were a lot bigger than we were and that was good enough reason for Morris. The loss of his potential profits selling the balls back to the golfers didn't seem to bother him. It didn't bother me much either, but then again I would have felt ashamed encroaching on their business; guilt screws you up that way.

The part-Cree kids could talk with their mouths full; in fact they didn't even have to sit at the table to eat but grabbed a handful of potato or a chunk of fish whenever they were hungry, and if their parents even noticed, they would simply smile. Morris could go to bed when he was tired and stay up if he was not, a sensible arrangement, I thought. He could wear what he wanted to, including gum boots. I wanted gum boots so bad I could taste it, but my parents said I should wear proper shoes. Shoes! In the country in Manitoba?!

We played kick-the-can every night through May that spring, and the part-Cree kids were the best at sneaking up when your back was turned and freeing everybody you'd worked so hard to catch. Morris taught me how to smear dirt on my face so I wasn't so easy to see staring out of my hiding place. We'd hide together, one on each side of a chicken coop or a reaper so if "It" got close to one of us, that one would come out in the open and argue with "It" over some obscure point in the game while the other would run and kick the can.

Those part-Cree kids played hard, laughed easily, fought to win. Like Morris. They yelled and danced and played good hockey all weekend on the rink they cleared on the ice in the middle of the river. They could run like the wind and sing strange music, like Morris. They could be hurt by friends and get sick and grow feverish and die with galloping pneumonia. Like my best friend Morris. Who hit me in the eye when I said something thoughtless about his family or his house or something I don't remember. I don't even think I knew what I'd said to hurt him the day he came to my place while I was building a snow fort and he poked me in the eye with his small fist. He didn't like me any more, he said, and wouldn't play with me any more, he said, and then he died. Was it only a week later? For years I knew he had died because I was so mad at him.

What would Jesus have said of the careless remark I made to hurt Morris so badly? He would have called it what it was, unkind and demeaning and wrong. And then—as always—he would have forgiven me and expected me to do something for Morris. But I was too late.

I've come to the conclusion that guilt is only useful if we draw on the spirit and grace of God to change our attitudes in how we treat a neighbor.

*   *   *

Jesus spent a lot of energy defending the people who came to him wounded by guilt. Guilt isn't the fault of the law, he argued. The law was a good thing, a picture of what is right and wrong, and Jesus urged his listeners to see in the commandments the ideals of life in the reality of God. But some lawyers and politicians and power-brokers were guilt makers, who used the law to gain an edge for themselves over others. Everything good can be handled that way, used as a weapon to dominate others and draw advantage and privilege to oneself. In effect Jesus said to those people, if what you want in life is power over others, that will be all you get as your reward. And you will never know what you have lost.

This was the background for the beatitude-proverbs of Jesus and his sermon on the mountainside in Matthew's gospel. Don't walk over others. If somebody treats you as an enemy because he thinks you owe him a coat and thrusts guilt at you, give him the coat and your shirt as well. Be a peacemaker, Jesus urged, and you will go beyond the law's requirements to its real intent.

Peacemakers develop a skill as reconcilers, just like Jesus.

There is much more to reconciliation than what the Reverend Macdonald taught us kids in our Sunday School class. I grew up thinking that the reconciliation of Jesus had to do only with being forgiven of my guilt and sin so I could get right with God. But what we were learning in Frog Hollow was that being reconciled to God opened up a vast array of new possibilities, and that whatever remained of my lifetime called for me to work at reconciliation in my world—with family, neighbors, "enemies" perceived and enemies real, the environment, the body public, in fact, every element in the world around me. I was to "work out my own salvation," as the apostle Paul put it, by taking up my calling, the calling of every human under the sun, to become as Christ to the world, to be a maker of peace, a reconciler, a forgiver of sins/transgressions.

Is this a great calling, or what? "Blessed are the peacemakers, for they will be called the children of God." Reconciliation is what it's all about. Not living as hustlers in the rat-race, but as children of God in his total reality, as active peacemakers. And as a result of opening ourselves up to God and his realm, his grace is there for us— abundantly. As the gospel of John puts our evolution in grace, all who accept the new reality are given "the power to become children of God."

Jesus undermined the sin of the world and took away its capacity to defeat us. Furthermore, the same spirit, the same understanding, the same energy-in-grace Jesus knew is available to everyone. So what is required of us? Nothing but the willingness to practice—for the rest of our days—being another "child of God."

Then guilt becomes just what it is, an opportunity for reconciliation and re-creation.

* * *

Guilt brought our neighbor Walt Gibson by our place the second time, when he came to ask if our dog was home. Since Shep lay asleep in the corner under the television, I just pointed to him and asked Walt to sit and visit.

A lanky six foot plus, Walt folded himself into a chair. He had retired from the army and bought a little farm along Joe's Creek. His wife still had a good job in Baltimore and wanted to hang on until she got her pension, so through the week Walt lived by himself while he fixed the place up. He built an addition to the house, repaired the barn, and fixed the fences. On the weekends his wife did a wonderful job planting shrubs and flowers. The Gibsons joined the church in the village and folks grew to appreciate them as neighbors.

So the first time Walt came by, it was puzzling since he was with Bill Deavers and both looked to me to be a little apprehensive. Walt asked if we'd mind if he set some traps on our land. One of his steers had stomped a fox to death and he worried maybe it was rabid, so he had it tested. The test showed the fox wasn't carrying rabies, but he thought there were more foxes in the woods on our land, so he wanted to run some jaw traps.

Norma and I didn't like the idea. Jaw traps are cruel devices and don't much care what steps in them. Bill huffed and shook his head. "I figured that's what you'd say. But this man's cattle's apt to get bit, then what? You want to be that kind of neighbor, go ahead."

Bill could lay a guilt trip with the best, and he knew just when to back off the pressure. "Traps would be down for a week, that's all. Could protect you and your family. Dog too."

Walt was learning, so he gave it the final twist. "You won't have to do anything, I'll do it all. You've got nothing to lose."

"But *we're* not going to put our feet in the trap," Norma

muttered, looking at me. I shrugged. She lifted her eyebrows and sighed.

I spoke to Walt but stared at Bill. "Only a week, Walt, okay?" I felt guilty agreeing but I'd have felt maybe more guilt saying no. Bill grinned at me. "That wasn't so bad, was it?" He should have been a shrink. Or a preacher.

When Walt showed up a couple of days later, I figured maybe he'd cleaned out all the foxes in the woods and it'd be my fault for letting him set his traps. But then he asked about Shep.

"Walt, why'd you want to know about our dog?" Norma asked as she put the kettle on the stove and got some mugs out of the cupboard.

Walt twisted in the chair and stuck out one foot as if it wasn't too comfortable. He cleared his throat again. "Bill showed me a groundhog hole he thought maybe a fox was using for a den, so I set a trap there. I set a couple others along the fence line too, where they might squeeze under."

"Did you get a fox?" I asked.

He looked a little sheepish. "Got two skunks. Guess maybe it serves me right. Haven't got the smell out of my mouth yet."

Norma was coming up behind Walt with a plate of cookies, so he didn't see her punch the air and mouth, "All right!" I fought a smile but she didn't bother.

Walt wasn't finished. "Caught a dog too. That's why I came to see about yours. Poor thing was whining when I came up, that's how I knew it wasn't a fox. Caught it by the foreleg. I don't remember much what it looked like; it could have been yours." He peered at Shep. "Except I don't think it had so much color along with the black."

Walt took a cookie and dunked it in his coffee. "I'm not going to set any more traps." He sucked on the cookie and hesitated as if he didn't know how to say what he wanted to say next. He dunked the cookie again and watched it drip coffee back into his cup. He took a breath then spoke quietly. "When I pried the trap open, the dog pulled his leg out and maybe it hurt extra much right then. He bit through three layers of clothing and took a chunk out of my leg."

"Then he ran off." Walt looked somberly down at his leg and rubbed the calf. "I guess I don't blame him much. If it hurt worse than this bite, I'd be looking to take some bark off somebody too."

Norma's sympathy for the dog didn't prevent a quick surge of sympathy for Walt. She pulled up a chair and sat down. "Did you need stitches? What if the dog's rabid?"

Walt nodded his head sadly. "That's the good news—no stitches. But I got to find the dog. If I don't find him, or if he hasn't been vaccinated for rabies, I'll have to take the shots."

We sat without saying anything for a little; the series of shots for rabies back then had an awesome reputation.

Walt finished off his coffee and stood up to go. "I'm sure glad it wasn't your dog, though. I feel bad enough about this whole thing as it is."

"I wish I'd never started on this trap business." He opened the door and stuck out his hand for a shake. "Probably isn't any foxes up there anyway."

Neither one of us could think of whose dog it might have been. There were a few strays that came around, but Shep mostly scared them off. We assured Walt we'd call if we heard anything about the dog from other neighbors. And we hoped he'd soon be feeling better.

He stood a moment on the porch, twisting his cap. "Maybe I'll talk to the Reedys, they might know something." He looked depressed. Guilt can do that to a person.

He nodded to Norma. "Thanks for the cookie," he said, brightening a little. "Guess I'd better go find that dog." He walked to his car, a little stiff in his right leg.

As she closed the door, Norma peered at me. "You don't need to look so pleased. I know you're happy the dog got away.

So am I. I hope Walt does find him; the way he's limping it'll do him good to see how much the dog hurts too."

"But I wish the dog had chewed on Bill Deavers a little for getting Walt started. Trouble is, I doubt if it'd do Bill any good. He'd never feel guilty about anything." But she was wrong.

NIGHT VISIT

10

Accepting Change

Like many of our neighbors, Bill Deavers had integrity. You could trust him, count on his word, take it to the bank. According to Jesus, integrity is one of the clear marks of righteousness. Another is humility. Most of us link humility with humiliation. But integrity turns humiliation into humility and makes it palatable. Much like Bill Deavers' beef.

Every year Bill butchered a couple of steers and sold them in quarters for people to freeze. I met him one day at Ray Hollar's machine shop; we talked while Ray sharpened the blades on my sickle bar. Bill told me his next steer was extra nice and did we want some at a good price? I told him I'd talk with Norma and phone him. He said to be quick, because he was butchering tomorrow and would hang the beef for a week in Marlin Burkholder's shed.

When I told Norma the price, she felt the offer was too good to pass up, so I called Bill, confirmed we wanted a quarter, and asked him when should we expect it. He thought a bit, then allowed it would be Saturday a week till he delivered it cut up, wrapped and frozen, and what size roasts did we like?

We settled on the size of the roasts, the number of steaks and how thick they should be, and how we wanted the hamburger packaged. I could taste the barbecued shortribs already, steaming with aromatic sauces piled high beside a mound of wild rice, with a side dish of buttered broccoli. Norma promised some of her great meatloaf for the first meal of hamburger.

So it came as a jolt when Bill showed up on our doorstep a few days later, hat in hand, looking as distressed as Walt Gibson had over the traps.

"What's the problem, Bill?" I asked, bringing him into the kitchen. Norma automatically put the kettle on and reached into the cupboard for coffee mugs.

"It's about the beef. Look, you folks don't need to take any at all." He twisted his hat in his hands. I'd never seen him like this before; he looked like a boy caught with his hand in the cookie jar.

"We hung the beef two days ago," he started. "It looked as good as any I've butchered before."

"Yet sometime yesterday, Marlin's dog must have chased a skunk into the shed. He sprayed around pretty good, and the meat picked up the stink. It didn't get hit directly but it'll sure smell; the fat soaks it up."

"Like I said, you don't need to take none." But Bill looked so downcast and guilt-ridden, Norma couldn't stand it.

"Don't you worry, Bill," she told him. "We'll take it and we'll eat it, too."

If possible, Bill looked even more abashed, yet hopeful; the unusual combination of emotions lit his face in a troubled smile. "Look, I'm going to trim the sides some more, cut the fat off as much as I can get at. Then we'll let it hang a little longer before it's cut up. That should get rid of most of the smell."

His face took on a harried look again. "At least I hope so. I sure don't want you folks to get skunked."

* * *

We don't eat much meat anymore. Some turkey when our family gets together, a little chicken soup for what ails us, but we haven't had a roast or steak for years. Bill's skunked beef took the edge off our appetite for red meat and brought about a profound change in our eating habits.

Yet all in all it was some of the best I've ever eaten, tender and flavorful, if you could manage to forget what you knew about it. Our daughter Debby and her husband Sam stayed with us for a weekend when their girls were little, and Norma made hamburgers and some sloppy joes and we had a feed of shoulder steak. Debby couldn't get over how good it was. We didn't tell her, at least not then.

Maybe there's an enzyme in skunk oil that tenderizes meat. The flavor was reminiscent of garlic, and certainly not identifiable as skunk—unless you knew. But we never got used to it, and red meat has never tasted quite the same since.

Norma has moved us over to rice, lentils, pasta and vegetables, with a little poultry here and there. This from a woman who developed the best lamb stew in the world, bar none.

Ask Shep, he's a food critic. He eats our scraps, and the stuff left from her stew was one of his favorites. Next to mushabooms, that is.

We picked up the word mushaboom when we lived in Nova Scotia for a time. It's a native Micmac term meaning "hair of the dead lying there," which seems an appropriate designation for road kill. Among Virginia mushabooms, Shep preferred groundhog, rabbit or possum to skunk—he has a discriminating palate.

Nothing seemed more toothsome to Shep than tar-fried

groundhog, flattened by a succession of cars into a hairy patty about two days old. He'd sniff it for awhile to see if it was done, then lift it tenderly by a stiffened corner and trot away to a secluded patch of shade and do lunch.

So now that even Shep has accepted Norma's vegetarian efforts with some enthusiasm, I've learned to like the stuff myself.

Change is a vital part of life, even when it's unexpected.

* * *

Like many farmers during the thirties, David Reedy's father kept a bull. Artificial insemination was then only a gleam in a veterinarian's eye, and with milk cows needing to freshen every year, a bull on the farm was a necessary evil.

Mr. Reedy's bull was a Holstein, as big as a prairie buffalo. David says Holstein bulls are known for their bad temper, and anyone with a grain of sense walking by his pasture kept an eye on the thing, because as beefy and muscular as he was, no fence would keep him in if he chose to run through it. But school kids don't necessarily keep the sense they're born with, and it seemed the Pellardine boys didn't have as much sense as some to start. On their way to school, they took to teasing the bull, throwing walnut balls at him to stir him up.

It got so as soon as the bull saw the boys coming, he'd paw the ground and make a run at the fence, bouncing along against it as he roared at the boys on the roadway. Even if he was grazing at the top of the hill, he would lift his big head high then go into a long roaring run at the boys as they passed on the road. The boys had stopped throwing walnuts at the bull and wished they'd never started. They were thoroughly frightened of the beast now and snuck along the road past him as quickly and quietly as they could, but the bull knew the boys and remembered he didn't like them.

One morning Mr. Reedy saw the bull charge the fence as

the boys went by and began to worry when the beast would make up his mind to go through it. He decided the bull must go before it killed someone; good neighbors think about the safety of their neighbors' kids. When David came home from his day job as a heavy-equipment operator, his father told him to take the bull to market on Saturday.

David doesn't remember much about the rest of his supper that night, except that it sat in his stomach like an old farm boot. There was never a question of refusing the job; on the farm back then a son didn't have a choice in chores if he was going to stay a member of the family. So that night, instead of sleeping, David worried through what he was going to do. The bull weighed close to a ton, and David figured he'd get only one try, because if he didn't do it right the first time, the bull would turn any second attempt into disaster. So he broke the job down into its parts; first, get the beast into the barn, next, get a rope on his nose ring, then load him on their old farm truck, haul him to town and finally get him off the truck into a stall at the auction yard.

David called on a couple of neighbors for help, but the bull's reputation got there first. Nobody wanted to play toreador, and David came home with one man's suggestion to shoot the thing in the head; as thick-skulled as it was, a bullet would only slow it up enough to get it on the truck. David might have entertained the idea but knew his father expected to get enough from the sale to buy another bull with a better disposition, and the only way to do that was to deliver a live bull to the auction. And this one was certainly alive.

David's brother James was the only one in the family who didn't make the bull restless, so David persuaded him to coax the animal into the barn on Friday night with a little feed in a pail. In the morning James fed the bull again while David backed the truck up to the loading ramp, then threaded a length of heavy rope between the front boards of the truck rack and through the barn door to the bull's stall where it stood, grumbling and snuffling in the feed bucket.

With James hanging onto the rope at the front of the truck, David picked up the other end, tucked it into his belt, then grabbed a three-tined hayfork and opened the stall. The bull pulled his head out of the bucket and started to shuffle as David tiptoed toward him, hayfork held out in front of him like a lance, tines pointing down.

The bull lowered his head and began to paw the floor, ripping great gouts of mud into the air behind him. His head dropped further, nose brushing the ground as he swept it from side to side. His huge muscles bunched, and David figured he was about to punch his ticket on those sweeping horns. David reached with the hayfork and drove the middle tine down through the bull's nose-ring into the hard mud floor, then hung on as the bull danced around until he twisted the ring against the outside tine.

As tender as the bull's nose felt pulling against the tine, David knew the fork wouldn't stay put for long, so he tugged the rope from his belt and looped it through the nose-ring into a tight knot, then hollered for James to take up the slack. As James heaved on the rope, David pulled out the hayfork and leaped over the side of the stall.

With both men pulling on the rope through the stake-side, they towed the bull onto the truck. David says the bull's live weight surging around in the vehicle nearly tipped it over until the boys got his rope snugged tight in the corner of the truck box. Then David braced himself for the drive alone to the stockyards. All the way into town, the truck rolled ominously as the bull tried to keep his balance.

When he got to the livestock auction barn, there was a lineup of trucks waiting to unload their sheep and pigs and cattle. The tumult of bawling and squealing filled the air with market-day sounds, yet nothing was making as much noise as Reedy's bull, now fully enraged.

A couple of the men in trucks ahead of David decided they'd rather be inside the sale shed restaurant than out where the bull was heaving himself around in the Reedy's truck, bellowing his fury. On the way inside they met the sale supervisor coming out; he'd heard the bull, too, and decided the best place for the beast was in a box stall, not out here where he could scare away the customers. So he waved David to the head of the line.

David backed his wobbling vehicle up to the unloading chute, then walked back to help the sale workers to open the tailgate—but none of them wanted to be anywhere near the bull. He could see them sitting on the top boards or peering through from the other side of the heavy wooden fencing.

The supervisor shrugged his shoulders. "That thing looks mean as a snake, David," he said. "I believe the boys are going to watch you unload him yourself...But wait a minute till I get inside. Good luck."

David laughed nervously; how had he gotten into this? He felt a surge of resentment at his father and brother; they were plowing and seeding a field back home in safety. This was something he had not asked for, did not want, and now could not escape. The whole situation had rushed at him, threatening his capacities. It had become a challenge to his understanding of himself that he had never faced before.

He beckoned to the men hiding in the stalls, but only one man climbed down off the fence to help David open the heavy tailgate. "There's a stall ready for him," he yelled at David. "It's back on the third row. He can't go anywhere but there; everything else's closed off."

David untied the bull. Nothing happened. The bull stopped bellowing, lifted his head, stared for a time at David, swung his huge head around to look down the chute, then swung his head back and closed his eyes.

The still silence grew, moment by moment. The men on the fences waited, squirming a little. David made a little gesture at the bull. The bull opened his eyes, closed them again and began to chew his cud.

David slapped the side of the truck. "Hey, get out!" he yelled and banged the truck again. The bull stretched his neck and rubbed his ear against the truck rack, eyes still closed.

"That old boy's gone to sleep," muttered one of the men on the fence. "Prod the bugger, we got other trucks to unload."

David took off his cap, gingerly stuck it in through the racks and whapped the bull on the nose. The beast looked up, turned his head and heaved himself around to the chute, ambled down into the alley and back to the open stall.

The men began to drop off the fence as David closed the tailgate. Two workers patted him on the shoulder as they walked by, as if to say "Good work." He waved his cap to them once and put it back on his head.

"I just did what I had to do," David said.

*   *   *

David Reedy survived the demands that made him a better man. He did not see them as experiences of evolutionary coercion. "Survival of the fittest" is one way to look at the idea of biological mutation. That may be an acceptable doctrine for the biosphere, and even for the long development of human history, but where would David's experience with his father's bull fit into the picture?

David's integrity drove him do what his father asked of him. No one likes to be put in a critical situation we have never faced before; the chance of failure is too great. Yet life has a way of thrusting change and challenge at us in ways we cannot avoid.

Jesus said something like, "Blessed are those who are pushed to the wall for the sake of their integrity, for the Reality of God is theirs." That's a wide-angled interpretation of "Blest are those persecuted for holinesses' sake, the reign of God is theirs," as one version of the New Testament puts it.

Jesus saw people making one of two choices: to do what gives us the advantage or to do what integrity demands; survival by selfishness or survival by righteousness. To take up the opportunity to "evolve" into a human being whose choice is the righteous Reality of God brings about actions based on integrity, honesty, and compassion. In our world it will take an evolutionary leap to change the hatreds and jealousies so dominant today. Only with newly possessed strengths drawn of God's reality can a person overcome anger enough to offer new forgiveness and mercy to an old enemy.

We *need* the disciplines of such a spiritual change. In the struggle to grow as "new creations in Christ," we will experience the grace of God in surprising ways, wherever we live and in whatever we do. That is, if we are poor in spirit enough to be a neighbor in the kingdom God is building.

How hard is it to "mutate" into the image of God? According to the history of faith, it takes the death of the old before the new can begin to emerge. This is what the symbolism of baptism means to many Christians; as the person is dipped into the water, she is "buried with Christ in his death." Then as she is lifted out of the water, she is "raised into newness of life."

And the great adventure begins.

MOCKINGBIRD

11

The Birds Speak

When we were first married, our perspective on reality depended on a lot of background: the impact of World War II, the friends we made in Manitoba, making a living, taking care of a growing family. We were far too busy to think about such things as the reality of God or becoming part of a new creation. I know both Norma and I had an awareness of God. From time to time some event would make us look at the world around us with surprise; it wasn't as it "should" be, it was out of joint, tilted, savage. At those moments—almost out of the corner of the eye—we'd catch a glimpse of God and *his* reality, as a light shining in the darkness.

By the time we got to Frog Hollow, those glimpses had settled on Jesus as Lord of that kingdom-reality, but it was pretty much a flannelboard kingdom of Bible stories and expectations. Frog Hollow was to transform the flannelboard images into substance and bring the Bible stories up to date. We began to see that there was much more to learn about reality and the integrity of God. And what we are all called to become.

Understanding Frog Hollow starts with the people and

their sense of belonging to something larger. The first evidence is in their appreciation of nature: poultry and beef cattle, dogs and sheep, deer and rabbits, trees and wild flowers. It's a matter of shared life; nature isn't there to be subdued but to be experienced, to be employed but not trashed. And there's so much life to learn from.

Living only with the pulse of business and the media, I had no idea how much we could learn from the Hollow's songbirds and their approach to survival. As a communicator, I became fascinated by the way songbirds attempted to manipulate their environment.

* * *

Mockingbirds are nesting in a cedar tree just off our porch. For some time we have suspected there was a nest nearby. Nesting birds are cautious with good reason; they are sitting ducks, as it were, for predators, egg hunters and nest snatchers, so reality and illusion are interchangeable necessities. Successful deception is a matter of life and death.

This pair are experts at manipulating public opinion, sneaking into the cedar by devious routes. Yet that is not all; once the eggs hatch, their skills at survival branch out and attempts to keep the secret are abandoned. When a hungry chick is hollering for food, the only thing to do is hustle for grub and forget the surreptitious flight paths.

Parent mockingbirds are about as exotic in their shopping as in their singing, with a diet that includes hundreds of different flying or crawling insects. But variety must give way to volume once the young ones hatch.

After stuffing a fat grub down her chick's throat, Mrs. Mocker struggles out of the cedar and flits to a branch of a locust tree. She sits a moment, like any parent after feeding time, wondering how to get out of the next one. Then she sees a grasshopper and reflexes take over. The mockingbird sifts down onto the grass and begins a wing-flitting dance that seems to mesmerize the victim.

Back in the cedar tree there is evidence that something is waiting. It has to be a male chick. The only other *enfant terrible* I have known that made as much "feed-me" noise per ounce of weight was our second son, popularly regarded upon the street of his infancy as The Noise.

The child's bellow could lift me out of a deep sleep, running. The only problem with a racing start from slumber is that the feet are engaged and the mind is not. Many a night I came awake trying to claw my way out of the clothes in our closet, having chosen it with unconscious abandon as the shortest distance to The Noise. Just in back of my tweed jacket, I would remember sullenly that I must first turn left to reach the door of our bedroom before proceeding to shut It up with a cuddle. Or with the bottle Norma was by then busy warming.

So I can sympathize with that enslaved mockingbird. There are few moments it is at peace, moments purchased dearly with an outsized worm stuffed into the maw of its progeny. "There, eat it or choke," she mutters, teetering on the fence by the cedar, wings askew and bill open carelessly, gasping for breath.

A mockingbird is the most gracious bird alive, at least in the Shenandoah Valley. Nights in early spring are silvered with its magnificent song. But right now, this one is paying for that midnight madness.

"Skreek, skreek, skreek." Away it goes again. The bottomless pit is in need. Some day that petulant gripe will fill our nights with stardust.

But in the meantime, Mother Mocker is too tired to even whimper.

* * *

Deviousness means survival at nesting time. Not the outright lie. Not even a starling can be a liar. I can think of several hoary names to apply to a starling, but liar would not be entirely fair. It is more the Biblical practice of being as wise as serpents and as harmless as doves. Or not letting the left hand know what the right is doing, such as where the nest is located.

The first year that we put up a nesting box for the Carolina wrens who were scouting the place, we goofed. I didn't nail it up close enough under the eaves of the porch. The wrens found the box, a 3"x4" house with an open roof. They found it to their liking, which filled us with an immoderate sense of oneness with our singing friends. Norma and I could see the box from the kitchen sink and noted the progress of construction with regular if not hourly observations.

Such industry! Laboring under a mouthful of timbers, Mr. Wren would fly in low over the lawn to avoid enemy radar. He would take a diversionary route behind the mock-orange shrub, up through the clematis vine and into the box. On another trip he would thrash in from the west like a helicopter hauling a television tower, thump his load into the box, then sneak out the back door through the wood pile.

A pair of robins were building a different kind of nest at the time, but relied on a similar gift for deception. Whenever one of us went out to the garden for some lettuce or a fresh tomato for lunch, the robins began their diversionary exhibitionism. "Look at me," one would command, "our nest is over here, where I am doing Immelmann turns. Don't pay any attention to the spruce I just flew out of."

Now it is true that these birds have not had the benefit of a course in advertising and public relations. There is too much Barnum and Bailey and not enough Hidden Persuasion in their efforts. But the robins succeeded in raising two sturdy young ones that year. Mind you, during the "hatch and feed 'em" season there was little time for finesse. On our trips to the garden then, Momma Robin would simply barrel out of the spruce tree and do a little ad lib threatening from the nearest fence post.

Not being fluent in robin dialect, we were ignorant of the insults and predictions for our children's children which were hurled upon our heads. Yet the imprecations served their purpose. We kept our distance and the fat progeny soon left the nest.

But the Carolina wrens, being smaller, needed to exercise more cunning. Due to my error, the first nest in the box was raided one morning by a cowbird. As is her purpose, she sought to fool the wrens into hatching a cowbird egg for her. The wrens are not ones to take such effrontery without a dust-up. Norma heard the fight and chased off the cowbird.

Too late. The wrens perceived what I had not, that there was too much space above the box. Instead of a narrow slit only a wren could squeeze through—even with a load of the best bluegrass—I had left enough space for an enemy three times the wren's size.

So that nest was abandoned. Not to worry. We have since learned that Carolinas may build several nests in different places. Since they have more energy than they know what to do with anyway, it seems appropriate for them to scatter a few dummy nests around while hiding the real one.

Nobody in his right mind would have chosen where they eventually raised their brood. In the tool shed. Through a hole in the eaves. On top of a roll of aluminum strapping. Beside an old flash camera. Behind my scythe.

For three years now the wrens have piled straw and dried weeds and orchard grass into the box under the eaves. And three years now their eggs have been laid in a nest inside the tool shed.

Last night when Norma reached in for the hoe, she nearly scared a baby wren out of its feathers. It was hanging onto the hoe handle, wondering whether it could fly if it let go. As the five-fingered apparition came closer, it decided to let go anyway and see what happened.

The next night we watched the parents coax it out of the shed. For the rest of the evening the chirrups of "Come on, fly over here!" could be heard all over our yard.

And once more the time of intense deviousness is past. Just the normal chicanery of staying alive remains.

* * *

Our understanding of reality is so often flawed, misplaced. Soap operas are real. Life is indexed to the Dow averages. Power is survival. Light is only an electric result, not a spiritual matter.

Yet later in his sermon, Jesus used birds to throw light on the working of faith. We count on our ability to bring in money to meet our needs, to the point that we panic when the flow slows. Birds don't panic easily; they're accustomed to finding their daily bread where it usually is. Without pockets, birds don't carry away an extra supply to store for tomorrow. So they trust and wait and do their bird responsibilities faithfully, whether finding food or wooing a mate.

In his first century letter to the Christians at Rome, Paul forged a link between creation and humankind that seems as up to date as tomorrow. Just as people of faith anticipate the reality of God moving closer, Paul said the whole of creation stands on tiptoe, waiting with us. People of faith are not controlled by greed or by their "sinful nature," Paul wrote. Instead they are moved by the Spirit of God, and Paul insisted that will make the difference between life and death, between the fullness of God and disaster, not only for humanity but for all of nature as well.

The birds of the hollow live on the edge of our lives, waiting. What we do in the next few years will determine which of their clans survive. Starlings and grackles and house finches will probably make it, but maybe the hummingbirds won't. So creation waits for us to take up our responsibility for their survival, too.

It's a tremendous responsibility, calling for all the spiritual maturity we can absorb through the grace of God. We not only have to figure out how to be good neighbors to other humans but to the land and its creatures as well. Big job. But as Paul pointed out, we have been made co-inheritors of the kingdom, so we have all the resources of God at our disposal. All we have to do is accept our responsibilty and act. God's spirit, his life-strength, will flow through us to bring healing, if we'll let it.

*　*　*

Do birds watch television? We're not sure. The two Carolina wrens who check into our spider plant every night—it hangs from the porch ceiling just outside the family room window—have a bird's eye view of our television set. They're not the best seats because the set's aimed toward where we sit, but the angle isn't bad, sort of like the left-hand balcony box at the opera.

We haven't been able to see which programs they prefer, but tonight the pair had the good taste to wait 'til *Jeopardy* was over and catch the start of the Dallas Cowboys– Washington Redskins football game. I don't mean to say Carolina wrens aren't loyal to the Carolina Panthers, only that their tastes are eclectic. Public television or commercial, sports or drama, comedy or documentary, the wrens take them all in stride. Or should that be on the wing?

It started after the first nesting period. Since the wrens usually build several nests, we thought the plant pot was going to become their next construction site. But after the first few days—rather nights—it became clear to us that this was not a housing project so much as an overnight motel. With color television.

At dusk, as any sane bird knows, it's time to knock off for the day. Sufficient is the evil thereof. No sense dragging a day out any longer than it's worth. Time to get your head down, under a wing if necessary. What we can't figure is, if these wrens were interested in sleep, why pick the noisiest spot on the hill? With a greenbelt around on all sides, why four feet from the television set?

Maybe they're just out of the nest. Kids who told Mom and Pop about the safe perch they'd found so the old folks wouldn't worry about owls and other night predators picking them off. But like kids reading under the covers with a flashlight, we can just see these two looking out from under their wings to catch the hummingbirds on *Wild America.*

Then again it could be an older pair with mature tastes; they do act like a settled couple. Nattering at each other as they close in on the spider plant, like, "You take the left side tonight, I'll try and smooth out the lumps over here."

For us it has been a privilege to be neighbors to such charming friends. We have many different species of birds in Frog Hollow, each with their own characteristics. Within a short walk we can see kestrels and bluebirds, veerys and orchard orioles, indigo buntings and red-bellied woodpeckers, among others. Hummingbirds visit the nicotiana and coral bells beside our porch. Downy woodpeckers compete with jays and mockingbirds for the suet we hang from a tree branch. Yet of all the birds, none are more appealing than the wrens.

One evening at dusk as Norma chatted with our daughter Cathy on the back porch, she reached out to an apron drying on a line between porch posts, feeling the pockets to see if they were still wet—and her hand closed lightly around a wren. It fluttered softly to announce its presence and winged away to a more private room for the night.

And come November, when we stack up some wood on the porch to feed our antique stove, the Carolina wrens get busy on any carpenter ants in the woodpile. When I chop open a cavity of ants and eggs, they'll pick it clean in a matter of hours. It's a wonder where they put it all, but with the energy it takes to flick tails, scurry around and scold as much as they do, a handful of ants couldn't last long. Or a woodpile full.

So it's nice to have their company in the evenings, just outside the window. As dusk falls, the pair flits onto the porch, chirring to each other. First one, then the other flips up into the spider plant, stirring the leaves like a breeze going by. Then stillness and quiet.

Time for a little television.

EMMY AND ROO

12

Horse Training

The question remains, how does anyone become an active participant in a new creation? How do we achieve the integrity of God and learn to draw on his presence? Gradually all our experiences in Frog Hollow began to suggest a new understanding. It is really as basic as our neighbor Ivy Moyers implies, and while she might not be able to explain the how of it any more than the rest of us, she lived its reality.

According to ancient perceptions, we are created to be in God's image. Yet God isn't a warm-blooded mammal like we are. So if we are to be like him, it must be in the essence of human-ness we call soul or spirit or psyche, as difficult as these are to comprehend. I am neither psychologist nor spiritualist, so I must labor to understand this most mysterious aspect of our lives without benefit of those disciplines. And I am convinced that inside, where the personality is formed, is where the image of God takes shape in all of us.

But without our willing participation, it is an undeveloped image, unexercised. God's image in us is not like a fetus in the womb, separate from the rest of the mother's being. Rather it is a pervasive vitality of life, an element of reality in that deep undergirding of our lives that remains dormant until we realize its presence, realize it *is* God's presence, and begin to come alive in a new way. To become aware of God's reality —in us and reaching beyond us—is a new birth, a stirring in our lives of the power and focus of life itself.

And that is just the beginning of our awakened, resurrected and evolving life. It is a life to be fully explored, a reality with new disciplines, new ways of functioning, new "laws" by which it operates. And we only learn about this life by experience.

I didn't realize how much experience I could gain from a horse.

*   *   *

Our daughter Cathy loves horses and has done so since she was a filly herself. She has her Horsemasters' Certificate from the Potomac Institute and keeps enough horses to teach riding. She has taught classes for the county and a local college as well as private lessons, so she wants school horses with a gentle temperament and good action. Some horses have a rough gait and every step jars your spine right up through your teeth; a beginning student can't learn anything if all she can do is hang on to the saddle. So Cathy looked for horses with a ride like a rocking chair.

She tried breeding some mares to Taraki, the purebred Arabian bay she co-owned with a friend. Some foals turned out beautifully, while others were a disaster. One colt, Roo, came out of a standardbred pacer named Emmy Award. He should have been a beauty, because Emmy was endowed with a pleasant though intense nature and Taraki usually sired offspring with his regal calm. Not Roo, however. He had the disposition of a weasel.

Even professional horse breeders get a throwback once in a while. Roo earned his name, since he moved more like a kangaroo than a horse. There wasn't much hope he would ever make an easy ride.

Roo had the potential for Taraki's strength, but not his calm nature. He did not like a halter; perhaps he wished to be free to roam the desert as his ancestors did at the dawn of history. But he would not have survived as a stallion since he didn't have the "smarts." Science decrees that animals do not have the ability to think as humans do, but that does not explain what everyone who works with a horse soon discovers: some horses are a lot dumber than others.

When Roo was three weeks old, Cathy introduced him to his halter. I offered to help one day, so Cathy handed me a neck rope. When you catch a horse, even one as small as a foal, it's probably safer to use a neck rope to hold the animal while you snap the lead rope onto the halter. Cathy could have caught him easily herself, but she wanted to give me something to do; I know that now.

Roo was in the pasture with Emmy. It was a lovely spring day in Virginia, warm enough for shorts and a T-shirt. It felt good to be away from the telephone and incipient pressure from clients; everybody needs to play hooky sometime. Little North Mountain shimmered in the sunshine, while four crows played kamikaze tag through the oak woods beside the pasture.

We sidled up to Roo, Cathy shaking some oats in a pail. Roo wasn't into oats much yet, but he was curious enough to wonder what his mother saw in them, so he smeared his nose around in the pail long enough for me to slip the rope over his neck and hook the snap. If I hadn't got in her way, Cathy would have snapped on the halter rope, too.

While I congratulated myself on my dexterity, Roo lifted his head out of the bucket and glared. He shook his head. "Now then, boy," I counseled in a masterful manner, "just settle down." He whuffed some oats off his mouth and backed up.

"Hang on to him, Dad." Reaching around me, Cathy

almost made it with the halter rope on her second try, but when Roo backed, he tossed his head out of range. Then he swung round in a circle away from Cathy, stepping smartly on my foot as he twisted his hind end back into my hip. It smarted, as did my foot.

"Hold it, you little snot," I snarled with some heat, trying to reel him in with the neck rope. But Roo decided he wouldn't play, lunged into the rope and took off. He caught me off balance, so all I could do was fall along after him. He was a big colt. Once he got me leaning forward, running, he knew he'd won; as long as I couldn't set myself to pull him up, he was in charge.

We got up a pretty good speed together; he had me taking ten-foot steps just to stay upright, whipping along at the end of his rope. It was a balance between his strength and my pounds, or he'd have plowed me into the ground in the first few seconds.

Cathy yelled, "Let him go, Dad, let him go!" But I couldn't. Roo steered a course through some rock outcrops to add dexterity to my footwork, then suddenly ran out of pasture.

As Roo turned sharp at the fence line, he whipped me into the fence. I grabbed the wire as much to stay on my feet as slow us down. The wire dug a chunk of meat off my thumb, but the race was over.

Cathy came up and snapped on the halter rope, then peeled the neck rope out of my fingers. I could see she was struggling with some deep emotion.

"Didn't know you could run that fast, Dad." Her voice squeaked around a giggle. She unhooked the neck rope, then handed it back. "Want to catch Emmy for me? I need to put her in the barn."

I looped the rope around a fence post and leaned on it to get a breath. "No, thanks. This has been fun, but in a minute I'm going to go in and wait for the phone to ring."

*   *   *

The Amish are about the only ones who still farm seriously with horses, at least since the years before World War II. Back then, horses were still part of life on most farms, Amish or not. David Reedy owns three tractors now, each with its own character and purpose, but his father farmed the same land with a couple of teams.

The first year that David was old enough to plow alone with his father's horses, one of their big Belgians pulled a tendon and came up lame. The spring plowing had barely begun. The vet told Mr. Reedy he'd better find another horse, and told him about a gelding that Walker Myers had for sale.

Walker Myers lived over against the mountain, so after morning chores, Mr. Reedy and David hitched the remaining horse, a bay, to a wagon and drove back to see what Walker was selling.

"Make you a good team," Walker said as he led the big gray up to the wagon hitch. Mr. Reedy looked him over, ran his hand down his hocks and peered in his mouth. "Tell you what, Mr. Reedy, plow with him a week and if he works good for you, buy him."

The horse looked better than he expected, and Walker's offer gave him the opportunity to back out if the horse was a dud. "Let's hitch him up," Mr. Reedy said, and took the gray's halter as his boy reached back on the wagon for the extra harness they'd brought along. "I'll drive him over the hill and back."

The gray stood easy and the two men soon had him teamed with Mr. Reedy's bay. When they were finished, Mr. Reedy climbed on the wagon beside David and whistled up the team. And began having second thoughts.

Reedy's big bay pulled away as usual—it was a good work horse—but Walker's gray hung back in the harness, letting the bay do the work. All the way up the hill the gray let his partner do the pulling. Even worse, on the way back down the hill, the gray moved out ahead, letting the bay do the braking.

When the wagon pulled into the Myer's barnyard, Mr. Reedy shook his head gravely as Walker reached up for the gray's bridle. "I don't know, Walker, he won't pull his weight."

Walker's voice exuded confidence, "Don't worry about it, Mr. Reedy. It's just a matter of training. You willing to give him another try?" Maybe more curious than convinced, Mr. Reedy nodded his agreement. "Then drive the team out onto the road again and wait for me to give the signal."

Walker reached into his overalls and pulled out a heavy pocketknife, then walked over to a clump of locusts growing at the corner of the barn. Mr. Reedy stopped the wagon on the road, the bay pulling the gray along beside it. Walker came back carrying a long locust switch in his hands. Warning David and his father with a finger to his lips, he crept up behind the gray. He nodded and as Mr. Reedy snapped the reins, he laid the locust branch along the gray's haunch as hard as he could swing.

With a surprised whicker, the gray took off, dragging his teammate with him, wagon bouncing along behind at a brisk clip. David hung on as his father jounced on the wagon seat beside him. Walker leaned on the barn gate and watched them disappear over the hill.

Twenty minutes later the team and wagon rattled into view, the gray still pulling its share. As the wagon came to a stop, Mr. Reedy told Walker he thought he could use the horse.

"I still say bring him back next week if he don't work," Walker offered. "But I think he'll be all right now."

Mr. Reedy handed the reins to David, who slapped them once and whistled. The gray pulled out smoothly with the bay, both leaning into the harness together.

"Like I said," Walker yelled as the Reedys moved away on the wagon, "it's all a matter of training."

* * *

To a person awakening in the "image of God," reality training is sort of like a swack with a switch to a horse, or getting bounced off a fence by a colt; when most effective, it's unexpected and moving, and while it stings some, it improves the attitude. But that's not the only way to expand our understanding of God and his nature.

When Jesus told the crowd piled up around him, "You are the light of the world" and "You are the salt of the earth," most of his listeners weren't used to being described in such terms. Quite the contrary; in the eyes of the religious leaders, these were common people, at best uneducated rabble unfit to handle spiritual matters, at least unclean sinners to be avoided. In consorting with such rabble, Jesus gave his opponents the opportunity to accuse him of diminishing the Law and the Prophets, a charge Jesus denied vehemently. They did not understand his intentions.

As soon as Jesus told his listeners, "You are the light of the world," he went on to challenge their concept of right living: their righteousness must exceed that of the scribes and Pharisees, an impossible task on the face of it. "You shall not murder" is the law: Jesus adds anger and insult as equally out of place with God. "You shall not commit adultery" is the law: Jesus adds lust in the heart. He expands in a similar way on the legal position of divorce, on giving one's oath, and on seeking retribution. Then he gives them what amounts to a new commandment: "Love your enemies."

In this way Jesus defends the commandments as the righteous beauty of God. Until heaven and earth pass away, they will stand. Yet what he has done is to lift up the *interior* dimensions of the law and leave his followers as challenged as his critics. Under these reinterpretations of the Law and the Prophets, how could anyone possibly become salt and light to the world?

Ivy Moyers would have said it's easy to make it hard work, because we think we must do it on our own, as if his presence is not in us. We mix up our responsibilities. Like the song birds demonstrate, it takes practiced dependence on the presence of God to learn how live rightly. The only way to be more righteous than the Pharisee and the scribe is to put our own inner driver out of business and become accustomed to the presence of God as driver. And how to do that is as unique as we are individually.

Being a disciple of Jesus isn't so much our effort at getting it right as it is letting this nature, this presence—the same spirit that ruled his life—infuse our lives. Then the effort becomes putting ourselves at the disposal of the reality of God in us, just as Jesus did, a big enough job for anyone to attend to. As we stumble and fumble along the way, learning how God wants us to live, our emerging integrity will be filled out and graced with his integrity. Such integrity will shine in any darkness to show how the character of God works to bring his reality to bear in the human community.

As long as we draw breath, we will have opportunity to experience more of the life of God in us. And for each of us, there will be different lessons to draw from the events of life. Even the embarrassing lessons....

* * *

Misty, a brown and white Shetland pony, was the first of many in Cathy's stable and a beautiful creature, but like some Shetlands, stubborn and difficult to train. When Cathy was in grade seven, she spent most of her evenings out in the pasture working with Misty on a lunge rope. When the pony graduated to a saddle, Cathy found out how mean-spirited a

Shetland can be. Misty was a biter who would wait patiently for hours for an unguarded moment to reach back and clamp her teeth on a tennis shoe with a foot inside, stuck in a stirrup. Or Misty would appear asleep, eyes closed in ecstasy as Cathy rubbed her down with a curry comb, then quick as a snake she'd chomp down on Cathy's arm or leg or any chunk of flesh her teeth could reach.

Never abusive, Cathy would whack Misty with a roll of paper she kept handy, or dump water on her out of a drinking pail. I urged Cathy to take sterner measures. One day as I held the pony while Cathy loosened the saddle girth, Misty peeled some skin off my upper arm. In instant anguished reaction I bashed her on the nose with my fist—didn't faze her at all. I think you could have knocked Misty out with a club and she would have considered it fair exchange and then bite you harder the next chance she got.

Misty also refused to urinate in the horse trailer. She could hold it till she floated her kidneys, so on a long haul Cathy would ask me to stop the truck and we'd go through the arduous process of getting Misty out of the trailer, walking her around until she relieved herself, then wrestling her back into the trailer again so we could continue our journey. She never loaded easily; I think sometimes we half carried her aboard.

So it was a delightful surprise the first time Misty let go in the trailer. We were on the way to the fair grounds, about twenty some miles, and we had no intention of stopping to let her out. Needing gas, I pulled in at a service station—our old pickup didn't pass too many—where the pumps stood in front of the door to a busy convenience store with a lunch counter. The manager himself pumped gas into the truck and we passed the time of day. He looked into the trailer and admired Misty (she was a beauty) and then took the bill I handed him and went into the store for change.

Just as the man came out again, Cathy crowed from the

trailer. "Look, Daddy, Misty peed!" She danced back from the tailgate and pointed to the spreading pool by the pumps. "She's learned how to go inside! We won't need to unload her! Isn't she wonderful! Good for you, Misty, good for you!"

But the manager only saw the pool of urine by his pumps just outside his lunch counter. "Lord, look what that fool horse's done! Get it outta here! Now!"

The educational value of any experience depends on your point of view.

13

Getting down to Basics

All experiences, whether good or not so good, give us the opportunity to learn.

I don't know if anyone from the hollow enters the horseshoe pitching contests at the county fair, but there could be some—everything else goes on that week. All over the county FFA kids and 4H Clubs aim for the fair; young members trim sheep, fatten hogs, comb the tails of calves and finish steers. The boy or girl who wins the ribbon gets top-dollar for a prize animal. The best steer can bring over a thousand dollars, so the kids work hard to ready their well-groomed entrants.

Misty didn't win a prize at the fair; she took some bark off the judge when he bent over to pick up a front hoof. The man never said a word, but he had tears in his eyes when he stood straight again. Yet Norma had won a ribbon for some of her needlework and Misty had learned to urinate in the trailer, so it seemed like a day to celebrate.

Cathy chose a ride on something called the Devil's Dip— or maybe the Swirling Sweep—I don't remember the name, only the face. The thing had two-seater space-pods on the ends of long poles coming out of the center, like spokes on a wheel angled up on one side. The tipped wheel rolled slowly around its center while the space-pods whirled at a higher speed out on the rim. Cathy wanted to try it, if I'd go with her.

"Sure, let's go for a spin," I smiled indulgently. Norma said she'd go through the flower pavilion and we could find her there after our ride.

She looked me in the eye. "Don't get sick on that thing," she warned. I told her not to be silly, these rides are tame or they wouldn't be at the fair. I reminded her I don't get car sick even if she's driving, not the most tactful thing to say. But she smiled anyway, patted Cathy on the cheek and murmured, "Look after him. He hasn't grown up yet."

I bought two tickets and Cathy and I lined up with a group waiting for the Whirly Wheel to stop and take us aboard. As each car came to the bottom, passengers let themselves out as new riders climbed in. I suffered a moment's unease, as some of the people getting off the Crazy Comet looked a bit green.

Must be the light, I thought, and felt cheered again. Cathy grinned and bounced and chattered as we strapped ourselves to the seat. "This is going to be fun, Daddy. Look at the lights!"

I looked, as the Infernal Machine began its twisting turns. The lights of the midway glittered below us as we dipped and rose again, wheeling faster in a wide circle through the cool night air.

"This isn't so bad," I yelled, "like a wobbly carousel. Only no horses." Then the thing changed gears.

Suddenly I felt squashed against the side of the car, centrifugal force sliding Cathy against me on the up-hill side. Or was it downhill? My stomach spun out against my ribs and began to feel delicate.

"Daddy," Cathy's voice sounded a note of caution, "I think I'm going to be sick."

"No, you're not!" I yelled back. Uphill or downhill, she was inside and I was outside, in direct line of fire. The Twirling Terror hurled us faster and faster, and it was so much worse than anything I had ever imagined could be. I no longer worried if Cathy would be sick in my ear. I could only clench my jaw and hope the stomach would stay in place against the ribs; it seemed desperate to fight its way out of my throat.

How far will the cookies fly if I toss them now? The mind likes to gloat as the stomach churns. *Time slows down as the machine speeds up,* it added cheerfully, noting that we seemed to be going even faster, which meant the ride wasn't likely to end soon enough.

Tears spun out of the corners of my eyes. Nobody in his right mind would do this for fun—why did we have to celebrate that fool pony learning to pee in the trailer?

The lights flew round in colored streams, up and down, round and endlessly round. I remembered eating a barbecued chicken. Yes, it was still down there but growing bigger with every turn. The cotton candy was a serious mistake. And I could taste the candied apple. I tried a swallow but wasn't sure which way it was working.

Was the Whirling Dervish beginning to slow down? Yes, the sensitive stomach felt a lurch as the brakes clamped on, and a new problem arose along with my gorge. A new motion— slowing down—changed the relationship of stomach and ribs in a threatening manner. Acids and barbecued chicken and candied apple churned in a cauldron of slosh, now surging back and forth as the Ghastly Go-round geared down and braked, geared down and braked. I let go the idiot bar in front and clasped both hands across my stomach. I noticed someone beside me doing much the same thing—oh, yes, Cathy, poor kid, glad she didn't puke upwind.

Gradually the Gyrating Nightmare slowed to a stop and

inched around to let the passengers off. We were about half-way around the wheel, for which I was humbly grateful. When the car door opened at the ramp at last, it was just about possible to stand and climb out. But slowly, slowly, do not jiggle the innards.

Cathy climbed out carefully. I followed her down the ramp and we stopped at the bottom.

"Far enough," I muttered. "I think I'll wait here until my stomach catches up. You go on ahead."

She looked at me balefully. "I'm in no hurry, thanks."

It took a half hour for us to ooze our way, a few feet at a time, to the flower pavilion. Norma turned and stared. "You look good, both of you. I've seen white shirts with more color. What took you so long?"

Talking spoiled the fun, so neither Cathy nor I bothered to explain much as we inched our way toward the car park.

"I guess we should go home," I told Norma, "but I'd rather walk."

Cathy leaned against one of the few cars left in the lot. "I think I'll stay here. I don't want to get in anything that moves, not till next year."

When we reached the pickup, Misty whickered in her trailer and Cathy's maternal instincts quickened.

"Guess we better try, Dad. Mom? Can I sit by the window?"

*   *   *

If it takes a lifetime to move into the image of God, what can we pass on to our children to help them get a start?

I suspect the shape of much religious practice in the hollow came about as parents tried to wrap a package of understanding to pass on to their offspring. And kids have always compared what their parents believe with how they live, a risk of magnitude for both parent and child. It's one thing to urge a child to believe in God, quite another to direct that belief through a forest of doctrine. An attractive short-cut for a parent is to apply lots of pressure; like laying a locust branch to the backside, there's an immediate response. But faith is such an undeveloped muscle it could tear under that kind of load.   It would be better for our children to see us living out a few basics:

√ God includes all that we know of reality and more. His presence can fill up our soul/psyche and make sense out of what goes on around us, even a midway ride gone sour.

√ Compassion, forgiveness and humility give evidence of God's reality; spite, envy and mercilessness are denials.

√ Living in God's reality calls for choice, and commitment to our "evolution" in the new community, the new culture of God; it is a discipline for a lifetime of growth.

√ Mistakes, wrong turns and lapses are to be expected; the renewed choice to live in God's reality by heeding his spirit brings forgiveness and redirection.

√ The strength to live God's way, with God's life, is freely available to any human anywhere, anytime; it's a matter of choice.

Anything more is gravy.

* * *

Frog Hollow would be a lot bigger if it was ironed flat. Texans brag about big. But our neighbors in the hollows of the Appalachians swear there's more land in the mountains of the Virginias than a crow can fly over in Texas.

Mountain bikes iron it out a little. We acquired a pair of 15-speed bicycles, although most pedaling in our area is uphill, so we only use the lowest gears, with an occasional modest incline to remind us what flatlands could be like. Once we took the bikes in the back of our pickup to a nearby airport so we could ride on the level for awhile. Like Manitoba, it was flat as old soda on a plate.

Shep likes to go with us. Bring out the bikes and he skitters around like a pup, his tail going in circles. He might even bark if he figures we're taking too long to fill the water bottles and check our tires for air. But as soon as we get on the bikes, he's on his way.

Norma is first after Shep down the lane. Three old apple trees grow on the fence line, their branches arching over the roadway to give us deep shade in summer; their leaves are falling now. Underneath, blackcap raspberry canes reach through the fence; they will offer their delicate fruit again next spring.

Shep shoots out onto the road at the bottom of our lane, heading up past Ivy Moyer's toward the Brethren Church. Like any sensible dog, he heads uphill while he's fresh. Still coming down the lane, I follow in third place, ducking the quail Shep stirs up in his race to get the first half mile behind us so we won't change our minds. Shep likes to range ahead, combing the roadside with his nose for the latest situation report.

This morning it's good he hustles on ahead. Norma stops at the culvert carrying the spring branch under our lane. She has a finger to her lips, then points to the bank of the branch. A muskrat is cooling himself, legs astraddle the damp mud. He watches us calmly; we push our bikes quietly through the open gateway onto the road.

We leave the gate open except in fly time, when we close it in case our neighbor's heifers get fractious and try to outrun the horseflies. Fences take a hammering in fly time, and we'd have a yardful of restless beef if we didn't shut them out. But fly time is behind us now, so the gate's open.

Shep would be embarrassed if we told him he'd missed the muskrat, so we don't mention it. He chases one of Ivy's guinea hens under her fence; it's safe there with Ivy's pet turkey. Nothing on feet frightens that bird, as he's all too willing to prove; the thing's a menace. But between the guinea fowl's warning screams and a guard turkey, Ivy is strategically defended.

The turkey has never shown an inclination to attack bikes, and with mixed frames we can get off them quickly as the need arises. Which can be very quick sometimes. We keep an eye on David Reedy's dog as we pedal past his porch. Shep and the little off-white bitch circle one another on stiff legs; Shep has been neutered, but he's got a good memory.

Up on the hill by the Brethren Church we hit hard top. The little white clapboard building commands a view of the valley as far as Massanutten Mountain on the horizon. It's worth a stop today, a quiet moment with morning mists making islands of the hill meadows and fields. The red ball rising over the Massanutten ridge will burn away much of the mist, but now the serenity of this familiar scene fills me with its enduring peace.

Shep snuffles at a groundhog hole in the ditch. We drift down the slight grade toward the deep oak woods at the corner, and Shep reluctantly gives up his diversion; there will be others. The grade's decline shifts into a gradual rise through the woods; autumn leaves show the soft russets of white oaks against the richer wines of the black oaks.

As we turn the corner, the hill drops away in a breathtaking plunge that will take us a half mile before we need to pedal again. Shep's ears are flying back, his claws clicking as he hurtles along beside us. We take it slow to keep him company. A squirrel suddenly breaks across the road and races for the trees, and Shep at full speed veers to cut him off. Shep doesn't see the fence until he hits it with his shoulder; the squirrel is safe, but Shep is limping now.

That's why Shep isn't with us on our next cycling jaunt; he is still nursing a bruise, and we leave him fretting in the corner of the basement. We don't tell him we're going on a bike ride, but he knows.

Cycling lets us share the life around us. Birds can cope with our sedate pace; there are no reckless attempts by a robin to fly through a windshield. We can hear the warblers if we can't see them, be moved by the cathedral-echo song of the veery in the deep woods as we pedal silently by.

I've often wondered what the old timers think of us as we cycle past, going nowhere in particular. As Norma and I pump our way in low gear up beside Willard Shiflett's garden, the sun-dried old man leans on his hoe to watch us.

"Nice morning for a little exercise," I offer, feeling guilty I'm not on the way to work.

But Willard isn't going to bail me out and agree with me. He waves his hoe at the rows of old vegetation he is clearing out for next year's planting. "This is exercise." His nod takes in our slow moving efforts to climb his hill. "But that looks like a lot of work for nothing to me."

Around the corner the hill flattens out to a gentler grade past Leonard Dove's place. Leonard delivers mail along the rural routes, but he's taking a few days vacation to put his garden to bed for the winter. I am pleased to see his big black and tan hound is securely chained to an old post by his rhubarb, but just to be safe, I call out to Leonard as we stop.

I'll have to take the squeak out of the brake pads on my bike. Or maybe it was my voice, dry and scratchy after the long uphill climb. Or maybe Leonard stood up so quickly that his dog figured something was wrong. For whatever reason, the hound took a long leap at me and pulled the old pole out of the ground like a straw out of a milkshake. I jumped off the bike on the lee side and pushed the wheel toward the dog, his oncoming fangs looking as big as Sicilian stilettos. Leonard hollered and dove for the post as the dog dragged a swath through a stand of old corn stalks.

When Leonard caught the post and reared back, I didn't

think he'd made it in time. But then the black and tan changed ends, his head stopped short while his hind legs kept coming, and he bounced his butt off my front wheel.

Leonard didn't know what to say and I was still focusing on those fangs, so Norma carried the conversational ball. Leonard's garden looked clean. Did he get a good crop of beans this year? It had been too dry since last spring; we could use some snow this winter to end the drought.

Leonard's eyes began to see again and with his dog reeled in, he started to relax. He agreed some rain right now would be timely. He liked bush beans and had canned some Top Crop, nothing like a mess with some bacon to make a favorite winter meal, and how did our melons do?

On the way home Norma remembered Shep.

"If he'd been along, there would have been a fight," she pointed out. "He would have defended us."

"And that big hound would have eaten him alive," I replied.

We were both quiet, wondering at the sequence of events. After she let Shep out of the basement, Norma gave him a little of his favorite treat, powdered skim milk in water.

David Reedy stopped in that evening for a visit and he laughed when we told him about our experience with Leonard's black and tan. David has been deaf from birth; he reads lips well and although his speech isn't always clear, he communicates with a combination of gestures and spoken words. He showed Norma and me how he handles an aggressive dog. Or even a black bear.

First, he said, you have to get him to look you in the eye. David scrunched down, sticking his neck out to stare down an imaginary hound. He reached around and whipped a big white handkerchief out of his pocket, stuffed it in his mouth so it stuck out on both sides, then roaring a huge sound, he danced from one foot to the other, waved his arms and shook his head so the hanky flapped back and forth on his face.

He did it so quickly it startled us both. He stopped as we applauded his performance gleefully. He grinned back at us, putting his handkerchief away. "It works," he insisted. "Looks funny, but it works."

"Dog will go pssshhtt." He slid one hand across the other in a universal gesture of dismissal. He allowed it wouldn't have helped much in the sudden attack we had come under. "But take a hanky with you anyway," he advised.

BEE
YARD

14

The Pain Exchange

As our beekeeping friend Wayne Showalter put it, four bee stings in exchange for six and a half gallons of honey isn't a bad trade. Wayne grew up watching his father run a thriving business in honey, and he worked with his brother to develop their own brand, sold in specialty shops and grocery stores throughout the region.

Since we were using Wayne's honey for most sweetening at our place, he encouraged us to get our own bees; he wouldn't miss the money from the few gallons he sold us each year. We bought a couple of hive kits and put them together over the winter, then ordered our bees and two queens. The result was a pair of thriving colonies of Italian bees.

We followed Wayne's advice closely, starting with two deep-bodied boxes for the brood chambers in each hive. Some beekeepers in Virginia use only one deep chamber for brood. But two brood chambers would give us stronger hives, according to our neighborly expert.

On top of the brood chambers we added the shallower "supers" for the extra honey a busy colony puts aside. The "supers" would hold the honey we'd get to eat. The first year we still had to buy our honey from Wayne, who had over 1,000 colonies spread out over much of the central Shenandoah Valley.

Most varieties of apples, pears, cherries and peaches depend upon bees for pollination. Many orchardists have their own colonies, but since spraying for insects kills off the bees as well, they must invest in fresh shipments of bees every year. (Bees are bought by the pound. Three pounds are a minimum quantity for a hive but when you're new at it, they seem like all the bees in the world when they arrive).

So Wayne has an arrangement with a number of commercial orchardists. He moves his hives into their orchards after the early spraying cycles are completed. His bees enjoy the spray-free blossoming cycle, and in a good year will yield a couple of gallons of honey per hive. Of course, he has the problem of yanking his colonies out on short notice, before the spraying cycle begins anew as the fruit develops.

We only spray our fruit trees with a non-toxic oil, starting just before they bud, then maybe once or twice during the growing season—any more seems overkill. It means we get some wormy peaches and apples with scale. But we don't like the idea of the pesticides and fungicides you're supposed to use, so given the choice we'd rather eat around the odd worm or two, and peel off the scale.

With our bees checking out every blossom for pollen and nectar, even the old apple trees in the field below our house suddenly took on new life and bore heavy crops of fruit. Wild persimmon trees up on the hill above the house drew honey bees in clouds, and there's a silver maple down on the creek our bees went for early in the season. Since all but our front pastures have been turned back to woods and wildlife, hundreds of different wildflowers bloom from spring through fall, and the bees seemed to enjoy them all. Especially sumac, knapweed, white clover, mint, chicory—and thistles. Thistles have to be good for something, right? And thistle honey is delicious.

Norma has made a study of bees, even taking a correspondence course on beekeeping through Ohio State University. She found out more than she really wanted to know; there are terrible diseases and catastrophes that can befall a bee colony. The knowledge kept her in a state of anxiety and suspense for months afterwards. But she soon discovered that if reasonable care is taken, bees are remarkably hardy. And quite easy to live with, particularly if you smoke your hives before you go to meddling.

Which I didn't do the first time we went to put on a queen excluder and the first super. A queen excluder is like a narrow-slotted refrigerator shelf, designed to let worker bees up into the supers and back down into the brood chamber again while preventing the much larger queen bee from following and turning the upper honeycombs into inedible brood combs.

When I started to pry the hive cover off with a hive tool—like a small wrecking bar—Norma asked why I wasn't using the smoker. I thought I'd seen Wayne check the hives without smoke, so I told her we could get away with just lifting the cover to slide on a queen excluder and the super. Still, she thought, we'd be wiser to use the smoker, yes?

"Relax, sugar," I spoke with honeyed assurance. "I know what I'm doing. Just watch how easy it is."

Bees glue everything tight shut with propolis, a varnish-like substance they collect from trees. It keeps out intruders and helps maintain hive temperatures for curing the honey. So to get into the hive, you have to work things free first.

I pried one edge of the cover up and a few bees came out to investigate. As Norma lifted the cover, I popped the queen excluder in place. But before I could put the super on top of it, about a thousand bees piled out in threatened rage. Angry bees are impressive; there are no subtleties to their forthright attack, a beeline straight to the nearest warm body. And in spite of being totally covered from head to foot—including a bee veil and gloves—two bees punched their way through my jeans to leave fiery bites on both legs.

Under the circumstances, panic is an appropriate response. Norma had a head start, but I passed her before she reached the gate above our house. Inflamed by two stings of her own, Norma pointed out with some asperity that we were lucky if foolish; in a few minutes we were able to go back to the hive and, using smoke this time, finish the job.

What did I learn from the experience? Not to be so sure I knew what I was doing. What did Norma learn? Probably the same thing. Humility was never one of my assets, which explains why I enjoy so many humiliating events.

*   *   *

Suitably reminded, I've used a smoker ever since. This is a tin can with a built-in bellows to squeeze air through some smoldering binder twine, burlap or dry grass, producing strong puffs of smoke. Some biologists believe the bees react to the threat of fire by taking on honey, perhaps in readiness for a move to a safer hive. In any event the bees are preoccupied by the smoke. They become docile and can be disturbed without much of a confrontation.

That season we pulled three honey-loaded supers off our first hive, without another sting. As I pried each frame of honeycomb loose from the super, Norma swept the bees off the frames with a bee brush. Then she put the frames in an extra super we brought along in our garden cart.

Back in the house, we took the beeswax caps off the comb with capping knives. Shaped something like trowels, the knives are kept hot and clean in a pan of near-boiling water. You can buy electric capping knives, but they cost much more.

Then we put the frames in an extractor Norma bought from a neighbor who gave up keeping bees. With it we can spin two frames at a time at high speed, as fast as we can turn the handle. The golden syrup flows out the bottom into cheesecloth strainers to filter out the beeswax.

One colony gave us five gallons of honey, above the national average of about four gallons. The other hive, only a gallon and a half. We puzzled over the difference until we learned that there are many reasons why a hive can falter; we suspect the hive may have lost its old queen and had gone through the struggle of producing a young new queen. The hive seems strong now, so we'll never know the actual reason.

For our first year, six and a half gallons of honey for four bee stings didn't seem a bad bargain at all.

* * *

We don't hear much about a back-to-the-land movement now, not like in the sixties. But it's happening all the same. A couple of generations ago when hippies flowered and communes sprang up across the countryside, people got the idea that "back-to-the-land" had been invented in the sixties. Since the hippies have now become yuppies, people think it's all over, finished, kaput.

Not at all. The love of land and sky, of fresh breezes and warm soil, of growing things and being a part of all growth continues to move the hearts and souls of many toward a gentle sharing of all life, an ever-renewed stirring which draws out of each generation those who cannot live in contentment apart from nature. So they take up the quest for harmony and balance, and discover the need for nature's forgiving acceptance.

It seems to me that the streets of the city do not teach humility in the same way as do the paths of the forest; the lessons of survival taught by nature are different and the experiences somehow more humane. Little wonder, then, that even in the city we turn to the heavens for our hope, to the land for our roots, to the rivers, lakes and seas for our renewal. While we may be dominated now by our own technology, we remain creatures of the earth, dependent, not independent. If we allow, the Spirit of Creation breathes life through us, in us, with us; the laws of "righteousness" become immutable laws of nature, of *our* nature. We may exist for a time outside those laws if we choose, but it is not image-of-God living.

*   *   *

Our own back-to-the-land attempt ran into a snag, as over a period of time and several operations, a malignant tumor on my left shoulder became a serious problem. To stop its progress, surgeon William F. Enneking took all of the muscle off the shoulder plus the top two inches of my arm bone, reattaching the arm to back and chest muscles. So it took a while to get back in the swing of things, you might say. It took more than a year to get used to working around the place one-handed, with the occasional assist from the other.

That second summer after my surgery had been one of those bone-dry ones we get in the valley, the pastures short and the winter hay long gone. We bought some hay to feed the sheep and horses, and I could one-hand that easily enough, but on the near side of the woodlot, a small glade had about a quarter-acre of orchard grass that looked too good to waste.

One evening after supper, I grabbed a sickle and started to cut in a corner of the glade. In countries all over the world, that's still the way fodder is gathered. The worker goes out with a sickle and a square of burlap, cuts some free grass along a roadside or on a rocky bank, piles it on the burlap square, pulls the corners together and swings the load up over a shoulder, heading for home and a hungry goat or cow.

As the razorsharp sickle sliced through the long stalks of

orchard grass, I thought, "This is getting down to the roots of reality." But the human body is not made to bend over and slice chunks of grass off at ground level. The first result is scraped knuckles. Second is a tightening of sinew starting at the thumb and running up through the elbow, over the shoulder blade, down the back through the buttocks along the hamstrings to the Achilles tendon and the toes. After twenty minutes I strummed like a bow string. Then I tried to straighten up.

That'll do for tonight seemed like a sensible conclusion to the exercise. There was enough for a good chew for a couple of ewes at least. *Let them figure out who gets it.*

The next day, still strumming, I remembered the scythe wistfully and how I could use it to slice off larger chunks of grass while standing up. *But it takes two hands, knothead.*

At that point Shep came to the rescue and showed me how I could swing a scythe again. As with most country dogs, he ate up road food and other delicacies from time to time, exposing himself to the possibilities of worms we'd have to treat. He caught my attention at that moment, skidding his butt downhill across the chewed over pasture, hauling himself along with his front feet. Don't mistake me; I did not see my answer there.

Then he stood with his hind-end over a short and strubbly locust shoot, chewed back by hungry sheep. It was just the right height and branchy, like a bristle brush, and Shep started to scrub his hind end back and forth over the top in a vigorous attempt to get rid of the itching strings that were driving him to distraction. Again, do not picture my resolution in such activity.

No, it was the synchronization that inspired my imagination. The smooth coordination of his two hind legs, waving and weaving his heinie over the locust shoots in an ecstasy of movement. I could do that. I could synchronize. Coordinate. Get it together.

I dug out the scythe, hanging from a nail on the back wall of the shed, behind the step ladder and a coil of brace wire. Under the work bench I found the sharpening stone. "Let's go, Shep," I hollered. "We're in business."

I grabbed the lower handle in my good hand and the upper with the other and swung a tentative swipe at the standing grass. The scythe sliced smoothly through its arc, and a swath of fodder lay on the ground. A step forward, another slice, another swathe. Six more and I'd cut more fodder in a few minutes than in twenty the night before.

"Thanks, Shep," I crowed, as I bundled the hay in the burlap square. "You've earned your keep for the rest of the year!"

* * *

Jesus experienced *real* pain when he was executed. Hanging by the hands slowly pulls the arms out of the shoulder sockets, sooner when you can't support your body weight on feet with a nail driven through them. So between trying to stand a little on a nail, then hanging with shoulders twisted out of joint from hands spiked to a crossbeam, the process of dying for Jesus stretched out over long hours in a great deal of agony.

Some people are turned on by someone else being hurt. Put people together in a crowd, whether watching gladiators or hockey players, and a little blood brings out a feral roar. (I grew up playing hockey, but I couldn't have been very good at it. I still have my teeth.) We like to take out the other side; it's them or us.

So it isn't hard to understand why, once Jesus was condemned to death and turned over to the execution squad, some blood lust showed up. Spit in his face. Whip him till he can hardly stand, then make him carry his cross. He is supposed to be king of the Jews? Push a crown of thorns down around his ears, then nail a poster over his head: "King of the Jews."

A lot of us are still trying to make up our minds about Jesus. Was he just another oddball looking for martydom, a rabble-rouser making it hard to carry on the business of surviving in the real world? Or was he our soul-saving link to a much greater reality, the "kingdom" that God is creating?

If he was a rabble-rousing oddball, then forget him; it's truly a dog-eat-dog world we live in, and we don't need a martyr to prove it. But if Jesus is our link to a new creation of God, then at least we need to investigate the reality he talked about and explore the way into it he described.

This isn't a matter of religion but of life, the kind of everyday, under-the-crunch life Jesus spoke about. Whatever we go through, whether humiliated in a bad relationship at home or crunched by circumstances on the job, we can slide deeper into our own defenses, blame others, react with lies and deceit, raise walls of anger and hate, and move further away from what we are meant to be in the image of God. Or we can turn away from such a self-oriented life to the fullness God has in mind for us.

Some choice!

* * *

The apostle Paul called it being obedient to the high calling of God in Christ Jesus: our willing participation in becoming a new creation.

It is an evolutionary change in human functioning *in which we participate voluntarily or not at all.* Furthermore, it is not a change we take part in unilaterally, on our own: God is involved from the beginning, even from the beginning of time itself.

The Bible never talks about evolution or mutation; the concept had not occurred to people back then. Yet the Bible is full of the idea of human transformation from one level of functioning to a higher one, always in obedience to a pulse of eternity beating in the universe.

The significance of the transformation is that it is from a self-centered, self-satisfying, self-aggrandizing life in all its subtle forms, to a life of love: a love so enveloping that God and self and others are wrapped up together in a new community of life, the emerging reality Jesus knew as the kingdom of God.

This community of life stretches from Abraham and Moses through Ivy Moyers and our other Frog Hollow neighbors into eternity and beyond, a community and kingdom deeply invested in whatever it is that God is doing in his universe.

For a reason, God's intervention in history has always called for honesty, integrity, forgiveness, mercy. In this alternate reality he is creating, he demands justice for all humanity, not simply for our own families and the people who think like we do. Furthermore, all of creation is to be included: the environment in which we live is to be cared for as tenderly as we care for ourselves.

Tall order. First of all, why should we give up self-interest in favor of the community? Or the environment? Common sense tells us that giving up our self-interest will lead to being walked on and abused. And common sense is usually right—that is, if we ignore God. But if there really has been an evolutionary process going on, if God has been calling human nature to a new level or "new birth," *then he is with us, no matter what we face.* When we put aside self-interest for the dangers and risks of community-interest, his presence is our ally. Not only is he our ally, but he will act on our behalf.

Even if it kills us. Life here is all that we know, and consequently it occupies the center of the stage; we don't want to give it up easily. But if we act according to a new nature, if we are a willing participant in an evolutionary movement fulfilling the image of God, we will have moved beyond life here and now to the forever of God.

Consider this: maybe God is seeding the universe with this new sort of human nature; it wouldn't be out of character for him to do so. There's a lot of universe out there to seed.

Whatever it is he is doing, it always starts here and now. We are here and now part of a growing host of people who have relied on his strength, his grace, his presence, to help them make the transforming leap into integrity and honesty and love.

That's where I want to wind up, in their company.

PASTURE MILKING

15

Young or Old?

Some days when I turn down the Frog Hollow road, there's a feeling of slowing down, a break from the primal screams of tormented technology, a return to the quiet sounds of nature.

An old friend of ours who ran a restaurant in town before he went blind used to complain about the noise levels at our place. "How can you stand the quiet?" he asked. He loved to visit, but was always glad to get back to the familiar roar of the city.

"People noise," he called it. Why does he prefer the city? Why does a New Yorker love the Big Apple? Beats me. Maybe there's a sense of security in all the humanity living right next door. Maybe it's the vitality of shared experiences, even a mutuality of anxieties, like how we love to hate a hard winter together.

The night life in Frog Hollow is stimulating, but in a different way. A chorus of restless, rattling leaves backed by an orchestra of crickets. The muffled thunder of a metal roof in a gust of wind. Owls coaxing field mice out of their nests.

The country is never quiet. A song sparrow trills on the

fence by the garden. A north breeze shivers the wisteria leaves on the porch. And if you work at it, you can sort out three or four cicadas, a crow in the distance, a chickadee in the forsythia by the shed and a timber truck climbing the mountain across the gap.

Maybe that's the difference our old friend notices. Only part of it is the noise of technology; the rest is the sound of unfamiliar life. Instead of night traffic and a siren's wail, we have the sharp bark of a fox. And the conspiratorial chirrup of raccoons.

About an hour before dawn, Ivy Moyers's rooster kick-starts the day. A cardinal begins the ritual greeting of the morning as first one, then another and finally a chorus of birds link their song with his.

Later the "people noise" joins in. Carl Bonner jounces by on his John Deere tractor. Mrs. Moyers's field gate squeaks as she goes through to her chicken house with the feed pail. David Reedy Jr. puts another piece of aluminum siding on his house, and the ring of his hammer echoes doubly from the facing hillsides of the hollow. An early jet hisses across the fading pink of sunrise. Over against Little North the whine of an orchard sprayer rides a tone higher than the cicadas strumming in the woods behind us.

Yet our old friend feels out of place when we bring him to the country to visit. Can't stand all that noisy silence and overfull emptiness, at least not for long. Serenity for him is tied to sidewalks and neighbor noise and action.

*   *   *

I remember serene evenings as a teenager biking with new friends on the streets of Winnipeg. The soft night air washing heat from the pavement as we flashed from island to island of light in the streetlamp glow, a cat racing out in front of us from under a parked car—why do they wait until you're right on top of them?

Around the corner at the Green Gables, high school kids gathered for as much serenity as a Wurlitzer cranked up to full volume would allow. The Green Gables presented awesome possibilities for me as an adolescent. Here the in-crowd met after school to exchange pleasantries, leer at girls and consume hamburgers and French fries (nips and chips to the natives then). Even to be seen in the place guaranteed one a sense of élan, a feeling of having arrived, an arrogance of belonging. For me, a recent transplant from the country and a year younger than most of my classmates, to be taken there by a friend was to put a foot on the ladder of social identity.

A neighbor, Herb Luckhurst, engineered the breakthrough for me. Herb was his own man, unflappable, low key, ready always with a well-turned phrase to suit the occasion. On the other hand, I was too much the friendly puppy, caught between loneliness and social naiveté, wanting to belong and wondering if I could, hurting for friends but unable to judge character. It's a dangerous state to be in.

Then there were the challenges. The in-crowd has a voracious appetite for new and exotic experiences. Nowadays it's drugs. But at the Green Gables, they held out for events.

I don't remember how I was conned into drinking a bottle of Worcestershire sauce on a quarter bet. It didn't taste that bad, really, nothing like the searing scald of a Jalapeno pepper. But the act created a sensation, and for a moment I basked in its glow. Until I heard a voice at the juke box, calling to a friend.

"Hey, Jed, you got to see this! Some clown's just drunk a bottle of 'Wooster' for two bits."

That was not quite the response I hoped for. A quarter hit the table with another bottle of sauce. "Do it again. I missed it." But by this time, stomach churning, I jumped out of the booth and raced for the men's room. Approval costs. Belonging can be a fleeting illusion, and the hunger for approval banishes any hope of serenity.

Maybe teenagers aren't supposed to be serene, even in the country. Yet serenity shouldn't be a factor of geography or age but of being right in God's way with yourself and your friends and your world.

*   *   *

We need each other. People who are exploring the reality of God need each other. The light on the hill is a city, a congregation of lights, not simply a lone candle. We learn from each other, from our mistakes as well as from our discoveries.

It's a little petulant to complain about the variety of religions and church denominations in our world. As tough as it is to sense and adapt ourselves to the presence of God, we need patience with each other in how we move into his life. Arrogance simply disguises a limited point of view.

We need all the help we can get maturing into the image of God. Events can chip away our misunderstandings of God, yet there is so much to learn about ourselves too.   Studying life together is a unique function of the gathering of God's people, and we're not going to grow as quickly without the concentration of experience we meet in each other.   Not all the people of Frog Hollow were members of a congregation of "awakening ones," but those who most influenced our lives were. Quietly and unmistakably, they demonstrated the reality of God in their own lives.

Of course we saw human frailty too. But then we usually saw remorse and repentance—great words, great experiences in themselves—followed by forgiveness and new growth. Integrity is powerful stuff, particularly as it rises out of the ashes of regret and failure.

* * *

Older now, supposedly wiser, and couched in the quietness of Frog Hollow, my spirit is still sometimes driven by anxiety. Tomorrow's problems rob today of peace, and I stare at serene Little North Mountain with clenched teeth and unseeing mind.

"My peace I leave with you."

Say what?

"Not as the world gives, I give peace to you."

Jesus, that's easy for you to say, but you never had a wife and four kids, a mortgage and income taxes.

"Don't blame me for your troubles. Lighten up. Loosen your grip on your life. Relax. Trust a little."

I know, you think I can trust God like you did. But that was 2000 years ago and a different world—now you want me to believe the knots can loosen on tomorrow's problems if I do what's right and compassionate and faithful today?

"You got it. Call it teamwork, if you like. As I said before, working with me isn't that hard to handle, and the work load we'll share is light."

Are you real?

"If I'm not, how real is anything?"

* * *

Is Frog Hollow a better place to grow old in? If the number of ancients living here is sufficient measure, it must be. But then there are a half-dozen young families now making their homes in the hollow, so is it, maybe, a better place to grow young?

It depends. The gray in my beard betrays a certain attainment of years, but not the way I feel inside. Why in all the talk of aging has there been no mention of the real truth? That if we are growing old the right way, our heads are getting younger?

Nothing is quite as old and rigid as a teenager who has let his attitudes and understanding be fixed by the peers he depends upon for his being. Except perhaps those "young" couples in their millennial 30's with a child or two. They seem to have aged at least a generation in a few years, certain that in the energy of their productive time the world has become their oyster.

But as the vitality of those intermediate years is tested, a happy surprise awaits: we don't need to get so old so quickly. We can be young again, for the first time since puberty, when "growing up" became such a cultural demand.

Remember how heavily it came at us in school? Our peers pressed the point upon us relentlessly. The dating game hammered the message home in those foggy fumbling years: "Grow up, be cool, get old enough fast enough."

Most of us never quite make it. And that's why we keep scrambling. As competitively as I tried in school, I was always at least six months too late for life —particularly after we moved into the big city when I was thirteen. I don't think I caught a breath until I hit forty-three.

Then things began to young up. Why do we try so hard? Psychiatrists and psychologists might tell us that it's because we haven't reached a desired stage in social achievement, or that it really has to do with our glands or how much our mothers loved us or didn't love us. It's nice to be offered a choice like that, and I've been wondering which one to take or if maybe there aren't a couple of alternatives these folks might have missed.

Like the man said, "Youth is wasted on the young."

* * *

Norma hopes Walt Gibson and his wife will like her cookies. I don't see why they won't. They're even nutritious since she bakes them with fruits and nuts and some whole wheat flour.

As any cook with experience will recognize, that is not an easy feat. Whole wheat flour isn't supposed to make a cookie, even when diluted with regular flour.

The '60s produced more than flower children. The dawning of Aquarius spawned a mood of skepticism among people who were too straight to drop out and turn on. The back-to-the-land movement may not have produced many successful long-term homesteaders, but it did generate the suspicion that we the people were being created in the consumer profile of the advertising agencies.

But never underestimate the determination of a born-again consumer, especially one who has had her consciousness raised by some anti-establishment books on nutrition.

"I am not going to bake any more crap for my family," Norma said demurely. "White flour has about as much food value as sand," she insisted, quoting her research. "I don't care if it's enriched with vitamins. The flour is dead, lifeless. The wheat germ has been removed, and bleaching destroys whatever food value there may be left."

Her first experiments in whole wheat cookie-making were sometimes hard to live with. A few refused to hang together and were best eaten with a spoon.

Others put marks in the floor when dropped. As in, "Oh, I dropped my cookie, now Shep will have to eat it." Poor Shep. The expression "tough cookie," formerly describing a mean gangster, now holds new value.

Still she persisted, experimenting with different mixes of flours, including one imported at no little expense from Montana, where some Aquarian advertising genie had been promoting an organically precocious whole wheat flour.

And now she's got the cookie licked, too, as our neighbors, the Gibsons, are about to find out.

*　　*　　*

This is real; you can't get ahead of the folks in Frog Hollow. Not that getting ahead of anybody is a virtue, but nobody likes to feel beholden, so when you get a chance to return a favor, you take it. Even if it's not really enough.

Lloyd Snyder came down to our place with his ladder just before Thanksgiving to climb up on our roof. He not only cleaned the leaves out of the gutters, he caulked some spots on the metal roof that might leak. Lloyd has done this for us repeatedly, and won't take anything in payment. Thanksgiving gave us the opportunity to give Lloyd and Liz and their two girls a gallon of chocolates, one small token of our appreciation for his neighbor-care.

As we've learned, it takes creative adaptation to be a neighbor. Until our children took over the Christmas celebrations, Norma baked a bonanza of cookies and gingerbread and peanut brittle and popcorn balls for our family festivities. She made enough to go around and then some.

She made enough to fill some parcels for our neighbors, just to show how much she appreciates them. I delivered a shoebox-full to Bill and Hazel Deavers. They had kept us in early lettuce when ours was still coming along. And Bill was always ready to loan us his tools and advice.

We didn't figure a shoebox-full of cookies would even things up. But at least they'd know we enjoy their friendship. Yet we can't begin to get ahead, not when I walk out the door with a two-pound slab of cheese Bill got for some beef he traded.

Same thing with Ivy Moyers. We have some of her gladiolas and dahlias among our flowering bulbs. When she heard we used old hay to feed our garden, she gave us her old haystack. And when she walks up the lane to visit, she often brings along a bag of something out of her garden.

So Norma packed her a parcel of cookies, wrapped it in Christmas paper with a ribbon around it and took it down the hill to Ivy's place. Ivy was waiting for her with a big parcel. As Norma unwrapped it, Mrs. Moyers explained how thankful to the Lord she was.

"I've got good health. And He lets me look after my calves. If it wasn't for my calves, there wouldn't be much Christmas."

Every spring Ivy gets a few calves from neighbors and raises them on pasture until the grass is gone in the fall; the income supplements her skinny social security, and lets her buy gifts for her children and grandchildren.

So when Norma opened the box of placemats Mrs. Moyers had bought, she knew how much it had cost her in physical effort. Rainy mornings when it would be a lot nicer to stay indoors. Evenings when a late spring snow piles up between her kitchen door and the haymow she must reach to feed those forever-hungry calves.

"But I figure it's a blessing to be active at my age." Ivy gave Norma a hug. "And I do love you."

The placemats show beautiful scenes of the rural countryside Ivy loves. Wildflowers in a mountain meadow. A birch-lined lane. Pine trees beside a brook. A quiet seashore. Maples in all their autumn color.

Each has a Bible verse with another "hug" of love. The lane through the birches quotes a psalm: "The Lord is compassionate and gracious, slow to anger, abounding in love."

I like the one picturing an Appalachian mountain glade, a sun-filled patch of meadow surrounded by azaleas blooming waist-high against a background of hemlocks. A verse from Psalm 104 urges a transcendent vision for our glitterblind eyes; "O Lord, how manifold are thy works! In wisdom hast thou made them all: the earth is full of thy riches."

Ivy's gift brings us something of her own abiding view of

reality. And we know again how priceless is her friendship. It's impossible to get ahead of the love around here, but it's nice to try.

* * *

What have we learned in Frog Hollow? It's impossible to summarize all that God has taught us through our neighbors, but a few things stand out.

We are never alone in the community of God. Everywhere we look, we find people who genuinely trust God and try in faith to walk in the new way of Jesus.

People on the way aren't there yet; arriving isn't the idea, it's learning what the way is like, and what it means to grow in the new life God is creating in us. So we'll continue to run into a lot of differences of opinion because our understanding is always a work in progress.

Beyond our differences and clashes of opinions and ideas, we'll find there is a host of basic understandings we can build upon about Reality. And since we are going to learn more as we go along, we'll need to be patient with each other.

What we know now and what we have yet to learn will connect in some manner with what we understand about the past, in the Bible and in human history.

On the other hand, some of the ways of explaining God's kingdom in the past will need to be updated as we learn more about his life in today's terms, with today's understandings.

And because we are different each from the other, we will continue to construct our explanations about Reality in different ways. That does not affect Reality at all, but it may cause us some confusion.

As we forgive our differences, we will tap an enormous resource for our future. The same spirit that motivated Moses and the prophets and defined Jesus as the Christ of

God continues to be our resource, building through us the purposes of God that we "see through a glass darkly."

And as the different grooves or trajectories in which each of us travel become more benign and less malignant, we're going to make it, as a species chosen of God for his future, and the future of the universe.

About the Author

James G. T. Fairfield has written in many genres, including a syndicated newspaper column; articles for naturalist publications; and books on conflict resolution, theological studies, and biography. He and his wife, Norma (a gardener, vegetarian cook, and illustrator) live in a century-old farmhouse near Frog Hollow. They have been married for sixty-three years.